W9-BOX-143

Praise for
The Unemployed Millionaire

"Some of the things I love and admire about Matt are his drive, his tenacity, and also his integrity. He's a young man with a mission to make a difference in the lives of people on the planet. There is a saying, 'judge a man not by what he does, but what he does that he does not have to do.' He's a young man that I'm just excited about knowing and working with."
—**Les Brown,** Professional speaker,
    best-selling author, and television personality

"The first time I sat down to meet with Matt Morris, I saw a man with an incredible vision. Partnering with Matt has been the single greatest decision of my business career. In the past two and a half years I've earned over $1,000,000 and traveled all over the world, and I'm earning a solid $50,000 per month in residual income that comes in whether I work or not."
—**Johnny Wimbrey,** Professional speaker,
    best-selling author, and host of *The Johnny Show*

"Just over two years ago I ended a business that had earned me a small fortune but required almost 100 hours a week, working all 7 days. I was looking for a way to not only earn another fortune, but to do it while having fun, traveling the world, and having time to relax. When I heard of Matt Morris and his success, it sounded almost too good to be true. I got Matt on the phone and asked him if I could fly to Dallas from London the very next week to meet him in person. After meeting him, I felt like we were long-lost brothers and I could feel his integrity and character shining through. I immediately started working with Matt and have had more fun in the past two years than I have at any time in my career. I've traveled to over a dozen countries including my homeland in India, been on safari, been on too many beaches to count, and cruised the Mediterranean, and I'm living my dream lifestyle earning six-figures-plus a year."
—**Kalpesh Patel,** Entrepreneur, London

"By following Matt Morris's advice, I've been consistently earning well over $15,000 per month in residual income for the past two years working from home on the Internet. Matt overdelivers to his customers and business partners in every way."
—**Stone Evans,** Self-Employed Internet Marketer

"In today's world, Matt Morris is indeed a rare find. A treasure. I'm ecstatic to have built a friendship and business partnership over the past five years. Because of Matt's mentoring and friendship I have advanced not only professionally but also personally. In fact, I have earned in excess of $250,000 just through my affiliation with Matt in the past three-and-a-half years. A BIG THANK YOU! Matt has mastered the art of 'putting people first.'"
—**Michael T. Glaspie,** "Mike G"

"I was a machinist for almost 30 years and had failed miserably in my efforts to become an entrepreneur on the side. Since learning the techniques Matt taught me, I've been able to earn a residual income from home allowing us to live a millionaire's lifestyle.... In the last six months alone, we've vacationed to London, Spain, Hawaii, Malta, France, and Italy. The best part about our life is that I've been able to be a stay-at-home dad for the past seven years!"
—**Ned Rae,** Entrepreneur

"Not long after 09/11/01, I was 36 and found myself at an all-time low in every area of my life. I had lost my home.... The company I was working for collapsed, leaving me without a career . . . and worst of all, my two young girls had just moved east to New Jersey with my ex-wife. I felt like a complete failure and for the first time in my life I got a glimpse of understanding what the handful of people in my life that had committed suicide must have felt like.

There was one person above all others who helped me turn my life around. After being mentored by Matt Morris, everything started to change. Within just a few months, I was able to give up the job I had taken and have been increasing my wealth ever since. Because of Matt's teachings, I've been earning a six-figure residual income for the past four years.... I own five acres in Colorado.... I'm living in a wonderful condo in Philadelphia with a fabulous view... and most importantly, I now have all the time I want to spend with my two daughters"
—**Chris Kinney,** Entrepreneur

"I've had the privilege of knowing and learning from Matt Morris for the past several years. The business and success knowledge he shares with me is always valuable and continually opens my eyes to new ways of thinking. Just one idea I acted on has turned into more than $40,000 (and growing) of passive income."
—**Kevin Wilke,** Cofounder, Nitro Marketing

"At the end of 2006 my life had hit rock bottom. My last business venture had failed unexpectedly and I had no income to support my family. I found Matt Morris and his success system in January of 2007 and my life is now at an all-time high. I am writing this testimonial from my new dream home at the Michelangelo Towers, Sandton, Johannesburg, the most prestigious high-rise condo in South Africa. I went from zero income in January 2007 to earning a six-figure income in just 18 months thanks to Matt Morris! If anyone gets their hands on Matt's business strategies, they have a winning formula when they implement what they learn. I am living proof that his strategies work!"
—**Soojay Devraj,** Entrepreneur, South Africa

THE
Unemployed
MILLIONAIRE

THE
Unemployed
MILLIONAIRE

Escape the Rat Race,
Fire Your Boss, and
Live Life on YOUR Terms!

MATT MORRIS

WILEY

John Wiley & Sons, Inc.

Copyright © 2009 by Matt Morris. All rights reserved.

Published by John Wiley & Sons, Inc., Hoboken, New Jersey.
Published simultaneously in Canada.

No part of this publication may be reproduced, stored in a retrieval system, or transmitted in any form or by any means, electronic, mechanical, photocopying, recording, scanning, or otherwise, except as permitted under Section 107 or 108 of the 1976 United States Copyright Act, without either the prior written permission of the Publisher, or authorization through payment of the appropriate per-copy fee to the Copyright Clearance Center, Inc., 222 Rosewood Drive, Danvers, MA 01923, (978) 750-8400, fax (978) 646-8600, or on the web at www.copyright.com. Requests to the Publisher for permission should be addressed to the Permissions Department, John Wiley & Sons, Inc., 111 River Street, Hoboken, NJ 07030, (201) 748-6011, fax (201) 748-6008, or online at http://www.wiley.com/go/permissions.

Limit of Liability/Disclaimer of Warranty: While the publisher and author have used their best efforts in preparing this book, they make no representations or warranties with respect to the accuracy or completeness of the contents of this book and specifically disclaim any implied warranties of merchantability or fitness for a particular purpose. No warranty may be created or extended by sales representatives or written sales materials. The advice and strategies contained herein may not be suitable for your situation. You should consult with a professional where appropriate. Neither the publisher nor author shall be liable for any loss of profit or any other commercial damages, including but not limited to special, incidental, consequential, or other damages.

For general information on our other products and services or for technical support, please contact our Customer Care Department within the United States at (800) 762-2974, outside the United States at (317) 572-3993 or fax (317) 572-4002.

Wiley also publishes its books in a variety of electronic formats. Some content that appears in print may not be available in electronic books. For more information about Wiley products, visit our web site at www.wiley.com.

Library of Congress Cataloging-in-Publication Data:

Morris, Matt, 1976–
   The unemployed millionaire : escape the rat race, fire your boss, and live life on your terms! / by Matt Morris.
      p. cm.
   Includes index.
   ISBN 978-0-470-47981-0 (cloth)
   1. Success in business.   2. Millionaires.   I. Title.
HF5386.M764 2009
650.1–dc22   2009015533

Printed in the United States of America.

10 9 8 7 6 5 4 3 2 1

This book is dedicated with love to the three most important women in my life:

My mother—Nancy Robb
My wife—Rhonda Salah Morris
My daughter—Zara Safia Morris

Mom,
You've been my hero and role model throughout my entire life. Your constant love and friendship is a dream come true for any son. My feelings are perfectly expressed through Abraham Lincoln's quote, "All that I am and all that I ever hope to be I owe to my mother."

Rhonda,
You've taught me what it's like to experience unbridled love and passion. You are my best friend and soul mate. Your love and support gives me the power to move mountains.

Zara,
Your birth was the greatest gift I could have ever received. You are the source of my greatest happiness and fulfillment. You are my shining light.

Contents

Foreword   Les Brown   xi

Introduction   xv

PART I
Building a Solid Wealth Foundation

Chapter 1   My Story   3

Chapter 2   Becoming an Unemployed
Millionaire   17

Chapter 3   Beliefs: The Easy Factor and the Power
of Lies   28

Chapter 4   Impotent Dreams Produce Impotent
Results   43

Chapter 5   Goal Setting Is for Losers   54

Chapter 6   Action Management for Peak
Performance   63

Chapter 7   The Secret Character Trait of the
World's Most Powerful People   76

PART II
Becoming an Unemployed Millionaire

Chapter 8　Starting a Business　　　　　　　　　97

Chapter 9　Why Invent the Average When You
　　　　　　　Can Copy Genius?　　　　　　　108

Chapter 10　The Ultimate Time-Leveraging
　　　　　　　Business　　　　　　　　　　119

Chapter 11　Internet Marketing　　　　　　　133

Chapter 12　Real Estate Investing　　　　　　173

PART III
Managing and Growing Your Business

Chapter 13　The Stress-Free Outsourcing and
　　　　　　　Management System　　　　　187

Chapter 14　Outsource Your Marketing through
　　　　　　　Joint Venturing　　　　　　　200

Chapter 15　Five Specific Strategies to Crush the
　　　　　　　Competition　　　　　　　　218

Chapter 16　Final Thoughts　　　　　　　　236

Acknowledgments　　　　　　　　　　　　245

Index　　　　　　　　　　　　　　　　247

Bonus Offer　　　　　　　　　　　　　254

Foreword

Les Brown

In today's global economy millions of people are losing their jobs due to sharp increases in technology as well as substantially cheaper labor prices abroad. Economic hardships, bankruptcies, and foreclosures have devastated people's lives and turned their worlds upside down. We are in a state of crisis. In the Chinese language, crisis means danger, but it also means opportunity.

In *The Unemployed Millionaire*, author, speaker, and entrepreneur Matt Morris has delivered a body of work that illuminates the opportunities in the midst of crisis. Inspired by the personal tragedy of losing his father and driven an insatiable desire to control his own destiny, Matt has written a book that is indispensable for this time and this hour.

Matt's frame of reference comes from years of concentrated study, having read hundreds of books and attended numerous seminars and lectures. In speaking about millions and becoming a millionaire, Matt is not only talking about money, he is calling on all of us to recognize the unlimited potential than we have within us to do more than we can ever imagine.

At a very young age, Matt felt the calling on his life to do more than work a 9-to-5. He may have been very much like you when he realized that he was not mentally fit to work for someone else for the rest of his life. He just couldn't settle for someone else determining what time he would get up in the morning, how long he would have for a lunch break, and more importantly, how much he was worth. Matt knew that he could do more and he had to find a way to make it on his own. Using the principles in this book, Matt went from being homeless and sleeping in his car to building a multimillion-dollar business that is changing people's lives around the world.

Many people, and you might be among them, are going through a mental transition, desiring to go beyond simple survival and even beyond success; eager to live a life of significance. In writing *The Unemployed Millionaire*, Matt unselfishly reveals basic principles and strategies that must be followed in order to achieve this level of significance.

Whether you have lost your job or are ready to create your own business, this book provides the master key to unlocking this new chapter in your life. Matt believes that if you do not have enough insight to realize that you have outgrown a situation and move on, that life will move on you.

For those who are hungry for a better life, Matt's insight will give them the ability to reframe their situations and see themselves not as being unemployed but as having been released in order to create their own financial success and pursue their greatness.

If your goal is to become your own boss, this book will teach you how to identify and evaluate the best business opportunities in this global economy. You will be armed with the specific information necessary to develop your leadership skills and the millionaire mind-set that is essential to make it in a volatile marketplace. With the knowledge you will gain from this book, you will no longer allow yourself to trade your soul and surrender your valuable time to a job you hate just to get a paycheck.

The Unemployed Millionaire is designed to teach you how to recession-proof your life. Each chapter will expand your vision of yourself and will give you practical, tried, and proven strategies that will allow you to give birth to the millionaire that resides within, waiting for you to tap into it.

I know from my personal experience of losing a job that it is natural to react with fear, anger, and depression, but you can't stay there. This book will help you take your life back and introduce you to a part of yourself that you are not familiar with—that is the millionaire within you.

This book is not for most people. If you have found yourself drawn to this book, congratulate yourself because you, my friend, are not like most people. The people who pick this book up are either millionaires or millionaires in training. If you are either one, you can use this book as a tool to carve out a tunnel of hope through the mountains of despair and create a brighter tomorrow.

What is your dream? You have taken a very important step by investing in yourself and using this book as a road map to take you there. The next level of your life is waiting for you, the world is waiting on you.

I believe *The Unemployed Millionaire* will be recognized as a masterpiece to be used to transform lives around the world. Join me and millions of others who have picked up this book and let's create an economic renaissance.

Introduction

We are all self-made. But only the successful will admit it.

—Earl Nightingale

Imagine waking up early every morning, five days a week, just to elbow and claw your way through rush hour traffic for the privilege of spending the next eight hours in a job you don't like. After being stuck in a job that keeps you from doing what you truly want to do, picture yourself fighting your way back home through rush hour traffic so you can see family members who know less about you than most of the people you left behind at work.

Now as a reward for all this aggravation, you get just enough money to barely cover your bills and a bonus of two weeks' vacation every year so you can taste a sliver of what freedom really feels like. Before you get too comfortable enjoying your holiday, you'll get yanked back to work where you can look forward to another dreary 50-week existence until you escape for your next vacation.

Does this sound like the life you want to live for the next twenty years? The next ten years? How about for the next five years? For most people, their job doesn't provide financial security, but financial insecurity.

Even worse, most jobs are nothing more than well-paid prisons. In prison, you aren't free to go where you want or live like you want because of physical barriers. In most jobs, you aren't free to go where you want or live where you want because of financial barriers.

As long as you have those barriers, you can never be truly free. For too many people, the only difference between spending life in a job and spending life in a prison is that a prison would give them better health benefits.

That's why I'm here to tell you that you don't have to live this way. Even better, I can also tell you how to get out of your current situation and turn your life into the life you always thought it should be.

In this book, I'm going to show you exactly how I turned myself into a millionaire before turning 30. If you think I had it easy or got lucky, I'll give you a glimpse into my life that will probably change your mind.

When I turned four years old, my parents divorced. A year later, my father broke into our home and murdered my mother's boyfriend by shooting him dead right in front of her. After serving his time in prison, he returned to severe alcoholism while my mom raised me, working two jobs with no child support and on food stamps at times, while working to finish her degree.

When I was 13 years old, my father committed suicide. When I turned 18, I decided to become an entrepreneur and by 21, I was such a miserable failure I ended up $30,000 in debt, homeless, and living out of my little beat-up Honda Civic, bathing in gas station bathrooms.

It was that moment in my life, which I'll share more about shortly, that I began to turn my life around. Based on the strategies I'll be sharing in this book, in less than three years, by age 24, I was earning a six-figure income, working for myself, and traveling around the world. By age 29, I was a self-made millionaire. Today, I have a business that has generated over 100,000 customers around the world. I've generated well over $20,000,000 for my companies by the age of 32 and feel like I'm just getting started.

Even though I'm a millionaire today, I still remember what it's like to be hungry and not know where the next meal might come from. I know what it's like to be homeless and sleep in the backseat of a car. I know what it's like to feel despair and discouragement and wake up every day wondering if life will ever get better.

I wrote this book to let you know that life can get better and it will get better; but only if you commit yourself to learning the skills it takes to create change. What pulled me out of a life of desperation and despair and into a life of prosperity and purpose were specific steps and actions that laid the foundation for success and ensured financial freedom.

The good news is that I'm going to share these strategies with you because I know they work. The better news is that I know anyone can do what I did and even more. If I can do it, you can too; and in this book, you're about to learn how.

Part I

Building a Solid Wealth Foundation

1

My Story

*The highest reward for a person's toil is not what
they get for it, but what they become by it.*

—John Ruskin

With fists clinched in frustration, I wanted nothing more than
to get out.

It was the second day of my marketing class at the University
of Texas and I was doing my best to focus on the drone of my
marketing teacher, Dr. Nguyen. He was a new professor at the
university who had spent his entire life in academia. Apparently
he flew through the business school with flying colors, but he
obviously cheated his way through English.

When he called out his version of my name, "Ma-chew
Mowis," he quickly pointed out that I wasn't sitting in my
assigned seat, established in the previous class. A seating chart
in college—really?

Not only that, he told us we couldn't even go to the bathroom
during class or we'd be considered absent. Suddenly, I was in grade
school all over again.

To my astonishment, he insisted I get up and move to the empty seat next to me.

Biting my tongue, I moved seats while I thought to myself, "Dr. Nguyen must surely be the biggest moron in the room." The fact that he was going to teach us how to be successful in the business world, even though he had never stepped foot in it, was a scary proposition. That was the first time the little voice urged me to "get out."

After roll call, he went into this long discourse on the importance of education and how those of us who wanted to get a good *job* in the business sector absolutely had to have a college degree.

"Strike one," said the little voice.

Then he told us how the job market had become so competitive that if you wanted to get a *great* job, we should get a master's degree.

"Strike two."

Finally, he told us that if we *really* wanted to climb the corporate ladder, we should do what he did and get a PhD.

"Strike three."

My knuckles were turning white and my whole body tensed up. Have you ever been in a place where a negative feeling takes over your body and you just have to get out?

You see, I had spent the last two years immersed in books about entrepreneurialism, going to every business seminar I could find, and listening to motivational and business programs in my car. I was also almost $10,000 in debt trying to launch my first business while "pretending" to focus on college.

Despite my initial failure, I was hooked. I was convinced I was going to be a hugely successful entrepreneur.

As I listened to this professor talk about how to climb the corporate ladder, I knew that I had absolutely no desire whatsoever to have a job and certainly no desire to climb any corporate ladder. The last thing on my priority list was working my way up to a corner office.

The frustration was so bad I couldn't concentrate. The professor's words started sounding like the teacher from Charlie Brown: "Wah wah wah wah . . ."

I wanted to scream.

"That's it!" the little voice said. "Matt, you can do it. College is costing you your *real world* education. You just started a new business and you need to focus on it. You don't belong here with all the other kids who are going to spend their entire adult lives being confined to a miserable life of 9 to 5, taking measly two-week vacations a year and trading their life away for a job. GET OUT!"

I was done.

I took a deep breath, grabbed my books, stood up, and walked out. I still remember the room going silent as Dr. Nguyen stopped his lecture, I'm sure wanting to remind me of the rule about no bathroom breaks. But he never said a word. It was a march of silence as I exited the room.

Maybe he knew I wasn't going to the bathroom.

As I stepped out of the classroom, I exhaled and a sense of freedom swept over my body. My college days were over.

After a straight shot to the administration office to cancel all my classes, it finally hit me.

What the hell was I doing?

I hadn't made a nickel yet in the business I just started, which was selling tax reduction educational courses. I had failed in the last business venture I started. I was about to turn 21 years old, had no marketing budget for my business, was $10,000 in debt, and had promised my mom, after moving back into her house rent free, that I would finish college.

I hadn't even left campus and the seeds of doubt were already creeping in. Would I make it? Could I really do it? Was I making the biggest mistake of my life?

But it was too late to go back. I had already crossed the line. It was millionaire or bust.

And bust I did.

The Bust

With what little I had left on my credit cards, I took out a cash advance to open a tiny 120-square-foot office since Mom wasn't exactly crazy about me running my business out of her house.

I had a desk, a phone, office supplies, and absolutely no one to sell my educational courses to. It was time to start advertising, so it was back to the bank for another cash advance.

I'll spare you the gory details, but after six months in business, my debt had tripled to nearly $30,000. I pawned basically everything I owned, spent 10 hours a day on the phone making cold calls, and still couldn't afford to pay rent in my office or at home, where Mom decided that since I was adult enough to be in business, I was adult enough to pay rent.

With all five of my credit cards maxed out, I was totally busted. It was time to get what I dreaded most—a JOB.

After scouring through the newspaper, I found an ad in the sales section that said, "Earn up to $10,000–$20,000 per month!" That was, by far, more than I had ever earned in a month. I thought to myself that if I had to get a job, I'd at least get one that gave me the opportunity to make a lot of money.

I went in for the interview and after a five-minute conversation, I was told that training started the next day. I was hired to sell above ground swimming pools. While I was nowhere close to being excited about the new job, I needed money bad so I figured I would make the best of it.

After the second day of training, I still hadn't seen one of the pools, which I thought was a bit strange, but they gave me a notebook with the sales presentation and I was set to go. Basically how the process worked was that the company would run a commercial on television showing a big happy family swimming in a pool and how you could get a pool for $400. When prospects called in, the operator would set an appointment for a sales rep to come out and show them a $400 pool, along with an "elite" version, which would be a bit more expensive. Of course, my job was to sell them on the elite version.

After training was over, they said they had leads all over the country and asked us if we'd rather stay near Dallas or go elsewhere. Because I was hungry to make money I told them to send me wherever I could earn the most income. They said the most leads were in southern Louisiana and asked if I could be there the following day.

So that was it. I packed up my car that day and drove to Lafayette, Louisiana the same night. They gave me a $200 per week salary plus commissions, which were to be paid after the pool was installed six to eight weeks later. Between my credit card bills and paying for gas and food, I had enough to stay in a motel one or maybe two nights a week, if I was lucky.

The rest of the time I slept in my beaten-up little red Honda Civic that had been wrecked twice. In fact, I had been rear-ended a few months earlier and was hit so hard by a big truck that my seat bent back. Even when it was in the upright position, I was leaned back a few inches. The hatchback window in the back miraculously didn't break, but the door it shut on was caved in and there was about a three-inch gap from the window. When I drove, it was like the window was down because you could hear the wind rushing in.

At the time, I actually remember feeling lucky for being rear-ended because the driver had insurance and I could use the $1,500 to pay bills rather than having my car fixed. That was my version of a lucky break back then.

Journal Entry—Friday, June 5, 1998

It's been a while since my last journal entry but with my new job I have a feeling I'll be able to keep it up more regularly since I seem to have a LOT of time on my hands doing nothing. I'm now working with a company selling above ground swimming pools. Basically, people call in to the company to buy a $395 pool and the company sends me out to try and sell them a more expensive $7,000 pool. I just started Wednesday evening so I've been in Louisiana now for a couple days.

My financial situation has gone from bad to worse and I'm in dire straits right now. I have about $200 to last me on the road till next week (Thursday). Between gas, food, and staying in a motel a couple nights, I'll be running on fumes by Thursday. I've calculated that I can

(continued)

> *afford to get a cheap motel room one or two nights a week*
> *and have enough to survive with my $200 a week draw on*
> *commissions. (Commissions aren't paid until the pool gets*
> *installed which is about 6-8 weeks out.)*
>
> *I slept in my car in a Wal-Mart parking lot last night.*
> *Tried sleeping in a cornfield first because I'm so cramped*
> *in my car but the mosquitoes were terrible and it was too*
> *hot in my sleeping bag. I woke up at about 9am feeling like*
> *I was being cooked from the sun beating down into the car.*
> *Note to self—find a shade tree to park under!*

For two months I lived out of my car and learned a few valuable lessons from being homeless. First, it was *not* a good thing to sleep late in the sweltering heat of July and August. Around 10:00 A.M., the inside of the car would heat up to about 150 degrees and I'd wake up feeling like my blood was about to boil and that I was going to die of heat exhaustion.

Another revelation was that by staying in a motel only one or two nights a week, one develops quite a bathing problem. After a couple days of 100 degree heat, I started to smell pretty rotten... not a good thing when you're going into people's homes trying to sell them something.

I learned to find gas station bathrooms that locked from the inside where I could bring my bar of soap and a towel, take off all my clothes, and bathe by splashing water on myself from the bathroom sink. The bathroom floor would be sopping wet when I was done so I always prayed no one would be waiting at the door to see the mess I had left them in the bathroom.

Such was my life.

Journal Entry—Wednesday, June 10, 1998

Slept in the car again last night since I only had about $30.
Get paid my $200 today so maybe I'll splurge on another
cockroach-infested motel tonight.....Ahh, the joys of my

miserable life. I parked the car behind a Kroger building w/ plenty of shade from the morning sun. It's gotten so hot that I can't sleep so I've been turning the car on every 30-45 minutes to cool off. I was doing okay until I got woken up by someone tapping on my window. Scared the hell out of me until I saw that it was actually a police officer. Evidently it's illegal to sleep behind a grocery store since it's private property. Not sure what they're worried about but I just apologized and drove to a hospital parking lot to sleep the rest of the night. Found a nice big tree to park under so I woke up without being cooked alive.

Hitting Rock Bottom

When you reach the end of your rope, tie a knot in it and hang on.

—Ben Franklin

Each night after my last appointment I would use a pay phone to call the home office for my assignments the next day. One night in particular after getting my assignments, I had to drive to the far side of the state for an appointment the next morning. After a couple hours of driving, I pulled into the little town I was going to work in the next day. It had been a couple of days since my last gas station bath and I had just received my $200 for the week. I was going to stay in a motel that night!

After driving around town, I quickly realized there was no motel. In fact, there was only one stoplight in the whole town . . . time to find a gas station bathroom.

After another 10 minutes, which is all it took to drive through the town another time, I realized there wasn't a single gas station open. It was late and I was tired and the next town was 20 miles away. I decided to just get through my appointment in the morning, hoping I wouldn't smell too bad, and then bathe in the next town.

It was raining cats and dogs that night as I pulled into a church parking lot to sleep for the night. I always felt safer sleeping in church parking lots than anywhere else. I figured criminals who might want to rob me (as if I had anything to take) might think twice doing it at a church.

I pulled in, kicked my seat back, and listened to the rain as I tried to fall asleep. But even though I was tired, I couldn't sleep. Have any idea why?

I could smell myself, and it was bad!

I knew that if I went on my appointment smelling like I did, let alone after another night sweating in my car, they would definitely *not* buy anything I was selling. In my infinite wisdom, looking outside at the pouring rain coming down, it hit me that I could just shower in the rain!

I took off all my clothes, grabbed my bar of soap, and stood out in the middle of this church parking lot completely naked, praying that no one would drive by and call the cops on me for indecency.

If you've ever showered in the rain, you've learned as I did that even when it's raining really hard, it takes a *long* time to shower because there's no concentration of water like there is from a showerhead. I said to myself, this is going to take all night!

Then my second stroke of genius hit me. Looking over at the church, which had no gutters, there was a huge concentration of runoff from the roof pouring down onto the asphalt. I walked myself under the runoff and had my shower!

After getting back in my car and drying off, I did some serious soul-searching. I was 21 years old, homeless, sleeping in my car, lonely, over $30,000 in debt, and bathing in gas station bathrooms— I even showered naked in a public church parking lot because I stunk so bad. Life for me that night hit rock bottom.

That was my wake-up call. I committed that night, even though I had no idea how, that I was going to turn my life around and become a huge success.

Journal Entry—Saturday, June 13, 1998

Just had my most interesting sales appointment ever. I was in the living room of the house, presenting to a husband

and wife when their little boy came running into the room holding out a puppy for me to hold. I nearly gagged, the dog smelled so bad—it was like he had bathed in his own poop or something. The little boy smiled at me as if he was the proudest little boy in the world. Smiling ear to ear, the boy yells to me "HE STINKS!" I said, "He sure does" and put the puppy down as fast as possible. The boy ran away and I looked over at the parents and they didn't say a word. My hands stunk for the rest of the presentation and I was dying to get to a gas station to wash my hands. I have GOT to get a new career!

The Turnaround

That night I listened to an audiocassette from Tony Robbins. It was a tape I had listened to before but it had gone in one ear and out the other.

One of the things Tony discussed was that we are all motivated by two primary forces: the desire to gain pleasure and the desire to avoid pain.

The pain I felt that night gave me the motivation to make a change in my life greater than I had ever felt. It was as if I was listening with a completely new set of ears.

In all honesty, I actually feel blessed that I experienced such a low point. I really believe that I had to feel such extreme pain in order to jolt me into making a radical shift in my life. The pain of feeling such tremendous loneliness, helplessness, and discomfort gave me incredible levels of motivation because I never wanted to feel that ever again.

You see, many people live their lives in a state of mere comfort. Life isn't great, but it's also not too terribly bad, so they just live out a life of mediocrity. They continue to go each day to a job they dislike, live in the house that's not their dream home, set an average example for their children, and essentially tiptoe through life quietly only to arrive at their grave safely.

> ### Journal Entry—Saturday, June 20, 1998
>
> *Have been reading what is probably the most motivating fiction book I've ever read, Atlas Shrugged. I'm less than halfway through, but took notes on a statement that hit home for me. "Man's greatest depravity is a man without purpose." Well, I feel pretty depraved right now since selling above ground swimming pools is definitely not much of a purpose for my life. I know I have so much more in me and realize this situation is short-term. I'll pull out of this rut before long, I'm sure. Need to figure out what that purpose is for my life.*

My Revelation

After listening to Tony's cassette tape that night in the church parking lot, I suddenly felt that burning desire deep in my soul to succeed. But I knew having desire alone is not enough. There were two things I decided to do to channel that desire into success.

First, I would adopt the concept of modeling others who had experienced the level of success that I desired for my life. The concept of modeling basically says that if you want to experience massive success, find someone else who has done it, figure out exactly how he or she did it, do the same thing, and you'll get similar results.

The second principle I adopted was a massive commitment to personal development. When I heard Tony Robbins's story of going from a 400-square-foot apartment to earning more than $1 million a year, I decided I wanted to have the same results. Tony claimed to have read over 700 books on success. He essentially immersed himself in the personal development industry.

Even though I didn't have a business or any other income vehicle at the time, I knew I could model Tony. If he read hundreds of books on success and then turned into a success himself, I decided I would do the same thing.

I read all of Tony's books and spent literally hours a day reading other books that would make me more successful in all areas of life. I read books on wealth, sales, communication skills, marketing, leadership, relationships, and many other subjects I wanted to master. Over the course of a few years, I read hundreds of books.

I started turning off the radio and listening to audio programs. I said to myself that no singer or radio show host was going to make me into a millionaire, but if I listened to audio programs from millionaire trainers, then I stood a much higher chance of achieving the same for my life.

My success didn't happen overnight, but what did happen was that I started making improvements little by little. I read an article on the human body that said every cell in your body regenerates itself every few years. This means every few years, your body grows a completely new liver, a new stomach, new hair, new skin—everything.

I remember thinking that if the human body can completely reinvent itself, then surely I could reinvent the level of success in my life.

I'd like to say that with my new positive attitude, I became a millionaire overnight and achieved a constant stream of success in everything I did, but life rarely works out that way. First, I had to dig myself out of debt and start earning a steady income. I still dreamed about succeeding in business, but now I knew that I had to take it one step at a time.

At that time, I made one of the best decisions in my life by getting a good, stable, and decent-paying job. I know this might sound strange coming from a guy writing a book on how to become wealthy by being unemployed, but I needed to get out from under my growing mountain of crushing debt.

When I was living out of my car, a friend of mine offered me a job with a software company based out of Austin, Texas. It was a good-paying corporate job that would get me back on my feet and allow me the income to afford a nice place to live.

Now don't get me wrong, I wasn't excited about working as an employee, but it did one major thing that was of vital importance. Because I had a solid steady income coming in, I was able to analyze my future from a stable platform rather than out of desperation.

Here's my take on having a job. First, your boss is going to pay you just enough so you don't quit and hopefully, but not in most cases, just barely enough to motivate you to do well.

I believe if you have a job, you should do exceedingly well and outperform everyone you can. I definitely believe that what comes around, goes around. If you milk your boss for your paycheck, you'll end up with employees milking you for theirs.

So during my time with this company, I worked hard and gave them much more value than they paid me. More important than the money was that the job gave me business experience and kept me afloat until I was able to develop my own business as an entrepreneur.

Let me give you one warning, though. Be careful not to get caught in the cycle of mediocrity. What happens when you're comfortable is that you end up getting deeper and deeper into a "good" life that prevents you from living a "great" life and accomplishing what you really dream about.

Although I still wanted to be an entrepreneur, I had become a bit soft wallowing in my "good" life and lost some of my motivation to reach for a "great" life.

Luckily that didn't last long because the company began having challenges and they laid me off, along with about two-thirds of their workforce (in one day). Although losing a job is never fun, it did teach me one important lesson.

There is no such thing as security in having a job.

So I was off into entrepreneurial mode again. Because of my job, I still had money in the bank that I could live on, but I never wanted to go into desperation mode again. That's when I had a choice.

I could have easily found another "good" job with another "good" company and probably lost it all over again sometime in the near future.

My second option was to start my own business on a full-time basis. Unfortunately, I had tried that route and wound up homeless, so I chose a third option.

I decided to get another job that would support me, but still allow me time to run and manage a business of my own. That's when I wound up working as a service technician for Starbucks repairing coffee machines. Pretty scary, since I had never fixed anything in my life.

I certainly didn't want to work at Starbucks for the money, because I knew how to fix coffee machines, or because I even cared about coffee. Instead, I took the job because their working hours would allow me plenty of time to run my business.

My working hours were from 6:00 A.M. to 2:00 P.M., which meant that I had the rest of the afternoon each day to concentrate on my business. After about six months of working at my job, my business finally started to earn me enough steady income that I had to face another choice.

I could stay at Starbucks earning a decent living from both my job and my business, or I could quit and concentrate more time on my business, knowing that the time spent at Starbucks was taking focus away from growing my business.

That's when I decided to quit my full-time job.

Since I wasn't quite at a full time income with my business yet, I still wanted the safety net of a steady income. I got a job working as a waiter for a nice steakhouse where I could work Friday night, Saturday night, and Sunday afternoon. This gave me a consistent income each week, albeit a small one, while freeing up my time so I could work on my growing business during the rest of the week.

Working a job and working on a business was definitely tough for a while, but in less than a year, by the age of 24, I was able to give up my job as a waiter because my business income had greatly surpassed my waiter income. Within another few months of being in business full-time, I was earning a comfortable six-figure income.

From the age of 21 to 24, I went from being homeless and $30,000 in debt to earning a six-figure income, being my own boss, traveling around the world, and living a life that was, at the time, my ultimate dream lifestyle. At age 24, I decided to reinvent my life again to become a millionaire. By the age of 29, I had accomplished that goal.

It took me approximately eight years to become a millionaire so it definitely wasn't a "get rich quick" process. It did, however, take me only three years to go from flat broke to earning a six-figure income, so results did come fairly quickly.

What I did was nothing more than what anyone can do, including you. Over my lifetime, I've spent well over $100,000 on books, audio courses, and seminars, and I have spent millions in business learning the hard lessons of life. In this book, I've taken the best and most practical ideas that have made the biggest difference in my life and to those I've mentored. With the principles and strategies I'll outline in this book, and of course your dedication, I'm confident you'll have the road map to becoming a millionaire no matter what your background might be.

I'm going to walk you through the major lessons I've learned, strategies that I've mastered, and pitfalls that I've fallen in through my journey to become a millionaire. I can't promise that if you listen to me, you'll become a millionaire overnight. However, I can promise that if you study this book and earnestly apply its principles, you'll definitely take a giant step forward toward achieving your dreams both personally and professionally. And that's something I guarantee.

Journal Entry—Monday, June 22, 1998

Back in Louisiana from a weekend in Dallas with the Marines. I was able to pick up one of my old paychecks from a temp agency I worked for briefly. When I went to the bank to deposit my check for $250, they had closed my account for hot checks and fees. After begging the bank manager who I had met before, he agreed to re-open my account if I paid the fees. So my $250 gave me a whopping $35! Guess I'd better start checking my bank balance before writing checks.

I can't believe my life has gotten to this point. I wish more than anything that I had a solid vehicle to put my efforts into that could bring me out of this hole I'm in. Feeling miserable and totally helpless right now. But I did just read a great book that lifted my spirits a bit.

I know it's just temporary and that I'll pull myself out. I've realized that no matter what I have to go through or put up with, I am committed to being one of the most successful men in the world.

Becoming an Unemployed Millionaire

You don't become in life what you want;
you become in life what you are.

—Les Brown

So what does it mean to be an Unemployed Millionaire? First, let's start with what this book is *not* about.

It's not about getting rich quick without doing any work. You can get rich and it can happen faster than you might think, but it usually won't happen overnight.

This book is not about filling your head with dreams of money falling from the sky or some lottery scheme to make you rich tomorrow.

Becoming an Unemployed Millionaire is not a walk in the park. You'll have to work for it, but the work can actually be fun and will be insignificant compared to the reward.

It doesn't mean cheating your way to the top or doing anything unethical. In fact, from my experience, long-term riches come only from total integrity. Being an Unemployed Millionaire is about loving who you see in the mirror every morning.

You won't be trading hours for dollars and working yourself to death. In fact, trading hours for dollars is completely against the Unemployed Millionaire philosophy.

Now that I've briefly explained what you won't be doing, let me describe what Unemployed Millionaires really do.

The core philosophy of the Unemployed Millionaire is setting up a business that generates income even while you're not working in your business. Rather than working "in" your business, you'll learn to work "on" your business so "you" can be taken out of the equation without your income coming to a screeching halt.

Let me give you a quick glimpse into my life as I'm writing this book.

As I mentioned earlier, I have a business that generates millions of dollars a year. What I didn't mention is that I also have a full-time staff of 18 people, a nice office in a high rise building, and even a big corner office overlooking downtown Dallas.

Here's how I'm different than your typical CEO. . . . Even though the office is only five miles from my home, I haven't set foot in the building in almost three weeks, as of the moment I'm writing this.

In fact, my wife and I just had our first child. Unlike most business owners who take a few days off (then it's back to "the grind" of 60-hour work weeks, only to completely miss their children growing up), my business continues to grow and thrive while I spend all the time I want with my beautiful daughter.

You see, I've created a business that's not dependent on "me." It's dependent on a solid business system that I've set up, which requires minimal amounts of time working "in" the business.

And don't get me wrong, it's not as if I'm absent from my business—not at all. I'm plugged in on a daily basis through phone and e-mail. But because there is not one part of the business that relies on me putting hours into the business, I have freedom.

I can spend the majority of my time working "on" the business, setting up joint ventures, communicating with partner companies and top affiliates, inventing new business ideas that will grow our business, and strategizing on new and creative marketing initiatives.

For me, "work" is such an incredible blessing because I'm able to focus my time doing the things I *love* to do, which I can do from anywhere in the world.

What being an Unemployed Millionaire is all about can be boiled down to one word—*choice.*

From personal experience, these are just a few of the benefits of following the Unemployed Millionaire business strategies:

- Taking weeks at a time off for vacations, any time of the year, all while growing your income.
- Freeing yourself from working in an office 9 to 5.
- Having residual income that keeps earning you cash even if you stop working completely.
- Having the time to spend all day at the park with your family if you so desire.
- Having the money to send your children to the best schools.
- Freedom to live where you want.
- Freedom to spend quality time with your loved ones and not miss out on the game, the concert, or the party because you had to work.
- Freedom to rise from bed when you want, without an alarm clock ringing in your ear.
- Freedom to avoid daily rush hour commutes that gobble up your valuable time by forcing you to sit in traffic.

In short, you'll have total and complete freedom.

This book is about taking back control and owning your life. Like anything worthwhile, achieving time and financial freedom takes work. But the effort is *far less* than a traditional job and the rewards are *far greater!*

Time versus Money

What separates an Unemployed Millionaire from everyone else is time and money. When you work in a traditional job, you have to give up your time during the day. Don't get me wrong. There's nothing wrong with a job for those who are not cut out for entrepreneurship. But if you've purchased this book, my sense is that you're either already an entrepreneur, or you're looking for a way out of the rat race. If you're wondering whether you should make the move to becoming an entrepreneur, let's look at what a job really gives you.

For most people, a job gives them money and that's about it. In exchange for that money, people sacrifice the best part of the day, five days a week. How much is your time really worth? Not only does a job trap you from doing what you really want to do, but it keeps you from truly enjoying moments such as watching your children grow up, spending time with your loved ones, or just being able to do what you want because you feel like doing it that day.

The biggest drawback of any job is that it robs you of one of your most precious assets—your time. We all have a very limited amount of time while we're in this world. For most people, they spend the best years of their lives being chained to the almighty dollar, having to trade those precious years away just to pay the bills.

If you add the amount of time you spend commuting to and from work each day and the number of hours you spend working, it's depressing to figure out how much time you actually use.

---

40 hrs per week × 50 weeks per year × 40 years of your life = 80,000 hours

1 hr/day commuting × 5 days/week × 50 weeks/yr × 40 yrs of your life = 10,000 hrs

90,000 hours spent working & commuting ÷ 5,840 waking hours in a year = Over 15 years of your life wasted!

Think about what you could do with an extra 15 years of your life. Would you want to become fluent in another language such as French, Russian, Chinese, or Spanish? Visit the Seven Wonders of the World and immerse yourself in the local culture? Perhaps you'd like to sail around the world, volunteer to build homes in South America, learn to salsa dance, take piano lessons, build your own airplane, or tutor underprivileged children. With another 15 years, what could you do to make your life more fulfilling?

Take a look at Table 2.1 to see the differences between an Unemployed Millionaire and a job. If any of these sound familiar to you and your job, you need to set a game plan to get out of your job and start moving toward becoming an Unemployed Millionaire, starting today.

TABLE 2.1 Average Person with a Job vs. an Unemployed Millionaire

Average Person with a Job	Unemployed Millionaire
Works in a 9 to 5 job	Works any time, can set own schedule
Sole source of income can be taken away at any time	Source of income dependent on easily duplicated systems that can be started up again at any time
Work may be boring, dull, tedious, or physically exhausting	Work is fun and exciting because it's what you enjoy doing
Well-paying jobs require you to work your way to the top after years of service	You set your own pace and can give yourself a raise any time you desire
Limited to specific locations such as company offices or geographical locations	Can work anywhere you are whether it's at home, while traveling, or in your favorite part of the world
If you quit working, you quit earning income	Your income is not dependent on you trading hours for dollars
Earns a limited amount of money every year	Unlimited earning potential— dependent solely on your own efforts
Retirement income lower than ordinary income and no guarantee that it will even be around at all	Income arrives steadily for as long as you want
Good jobs may become obsolete (auto factory jobs) or may need good timing to get in (working for Microsoft or Amazon.com)	Can be started regardless of current economic or technological changes
May require special tools or equipment only affordable by companies (bulldozers, mainframe computers, etc.)	Does not require any special equipment that isn't readily available to everyone

So if working at a job for 40 years of your life is not going to give you the fulfillment you desire, then what is?

Clearly, the path I'm suggesting in this book is starting your own business, which is the first step to becoming an Unemployed Millionaire. After all, how many people do you know who have become millionaires by working for somebody else?

However, be careful what you wish for! Just becoming your own boss isn't necessarily the answer if you don't plan your business correctly. When most people start a business, they wind up trading a job that gobbles up their time with a business that gobbles even more of their time.

As long as you love what you're doing, it doesn't matter how much time you spend. However, if you want to be an Unemployed Millionaire, you want the freedom to spend your time however you want, wherever you want.

With a job, your biggest expense is time. With a business, your biggest expense is money to set up your business and time to run it. As an Unemployed Millionaire, you want both time and money. You want to make your own hours and you want to make enough money to let you live the lifestyle you choose.

Unemployed Millionaires run their own businesses, but they also choose the type of business that gives them the freedom they crave. In most cases, the type of business you want to avoid are traditional brick and mortar businesses.

There's nothing wrong with starting your own restaurant or car repair shop if that's what you really want to do, but consider these problems. With any brick and mortar business, you must first spend money setting it up. This might include buying inventory, leasing a building, buying equipment, and hiring employees.

Once you've set up a business and spent a wad of cash, the next step is to spend time running your business. If you didn't like being trapped in a typical 9 to 5 job, running your own business can often mean working 10 to 14 hour days instead.

Even worse, a brick and mortar business traps you in a specific location. So not only are you trapped by the amount of time you need to put into your business, but your business also traps you in a specific location. For many business owners, they've simply traded the handcuffs of a job with the shinier and more expensive handcuffs of running their own business. To compare a traditional brick and mortar business with an Unemployed Millionaire's lifestyle, take a look at Table 2.2.

If you haven't noticed by now, you aren't going to become an Unemployed Millionaire by working in a job and you aren't going to become an Unemployed Millionaire by starting a traditional brick and mortar business.

TABLE 2.2   The Average Self-Employed Businessperson versus the Unemployed Millionaire

Self-Employed Person with a Traditional Business	Unemployed Millionaire
Works in a business that requires physical presence at all times	Works in a business that can run automatically without physical presence
Often requires working longer than 40 hours a week	Can determine the number of hours to work
Requires investment in building, inventory, or equipment	Investment in a building, inventory, or equipment is optional but not necessary
Limited to specific locations such as a company office or store	Can work anywhere you are whether it's at home, while traveling, or in your favorite part of the world
If you quit working, you quit earning income	If you quit working, you'll still earn residual income
Income often limited by the type of business	Unlimited income potential
Must save and provide own retirement income	Income continues to stream in after retirement
Dependent on local economy	Dependent on global economy
Requires having "hours of operation," limiting your free time	Can be done on your schedule whether during business hours or after midnight

In research done by Iowa State University that analyzed the effect Wal-Mart has had on small businesses, researchers discovered that in a 10-year time frame, small towns alone lost more than 7,326 businesses because of competition. In this 10-year period, Iowa alone lost:

- 555 grocery stores
- 298 hardware stores
- 293 building supply stores
- 161 variety stores
- 158 women's apparel stores
- 153 shoe stores
- 116 drug stores
- 111 men's and boy's apparel stores

Those statistics alone should be enough to have you realize that competing in the traditional brick and mortar business is almost always a losing proposition. As optimistic and motivated as you might be, competing against giants like Wal-Mart, Target, Home Depot, or any number of giants in various product industries is a tough battle.

Not only is such competition brutal, being tied to a retail location for five to seven days a week and working eight to fourteen hours a day is definitely not an ideal lifestyle.

What will turn you into an Unemployed Millionaire is starting a business that fulfills the following criteria.

- Doing something you love
- Starting a business wherever you want to live
- Starting a business that can run automatically
- Starting a business you can manage without physically being there

The first criteria, *doing something you love*, will make your business seem more like play than work. During the filming of the first Indiana Jones movie, *The Raiders of the Lost Ark*, Steven Spielberg turned to George Lucas and said, "Can you believe we're getting paid to do this?"

Steven Spielberg loved making movies, so working as a director never seemed like work to him; it seemed like an excuse to have fun with the biggest toys the studio could buy for him. Now let's see how someone like Steven Spielberg fits the model of an Unemployed Millionaire:

- Filmmaking is something he loves.
- Although film directors generally live in Los Angeles because that's where the work is, Steven Spielberg can now live anywhere in the world.
- After you make a film and distribute it, it can keep making money in theaters, through DVD rentals, and through television broadcasts.
- After a movie is finished, its constant sales continue earning Steven Spielberg money.

Some people might think Steven Spielberg is an exception or just happened to get lucky. However, the truth is that he didn't start as one of the richest and most successful directors in the world. When he began his career, he directed television shows and then progressed to movies. Spielberg was the classic overnight success story that took years to happen.

The point isn't to look at where Steven Spielberg is now, but where he started and how he got to where he is today. If you want to follow his success in whatever field that you're passionate about, you need to follow your passion. Passion will keep you focused on your goal and keep you moving forward despite people who discourage you and any obstacles that get in your way.

Before I get into the specific strategies, I want to spend the first part of this book helping you lay the foundation for success.

Just as a house built on a shaky foundation won't last, neither will your success if you don't create a strong foundation first.

Here's a sobering statistic. According to the Certified Financial Planner Board of Standards, nearly one-third of lottery winners wind up bankrupt. They lose all their money because of a lack of foundational knowledge on wealth and business.

I firmly believe that if you took all of the world's wealth and divided it equally among everyone, within 10 years those who were previously wealthy would again be wealthy. Those who were previously poor would again be poor.

You see, once you have a solid foundation on wealth building, you'll not only keep your wealth, you'll be able to do it again and again. One of the core beliefs I have about myself is this statement that I would like you to adopt after reading this book:

> *You could drop me off in any major English-speaking city in the world, take away all my contacts, take away all my money, require me to pick a completely different industry than I'm in now, and I have 100 percent confidence that within 12 to 24 months I'll be a millionaire.*

Creating your wealth foundation defines the core of your entire business career. To show you how to create a solid wealth foundation, I'll share with you the exact strategies that I used to develop my own wealth foundation, which turned me into a millionaire by age 29. Much of what we'll be talking about in Part I of this book is the mental game of success, or what I call your "inner game."

Far too many people live their lives with the belief that money is going to buy them happiness. Here's what I've found to be true—money simply makes you more of what you already are. So if you're a depressed and angry person, you're going to be more depressed and angry with money. If you're happy and loving, you'll be even more happy and loving with money. The key is to constantly build our inner game so we can build our wealth *and* our happiness at the same time.

Remember, true wealth isn't counted by the number of dollars in your bank account but in the intangible factors of your life such as your relationships, your memories, and your spiritual world. However, to get the most time and the greatest number of options for defining your own life, you need money. What I'm going to show you in this book is not only how to get the money, but also how to get it while enjoying an amazing and fulfilling lifestyle.

Beliefs

The Easy Factor and the Power of Lies

The only limitations for your life
are the limiting beliefs in your mind.

—Matt Morris

Most of us have gone to school for 12 to 20 years of our life to learn math, history, science, geography, and grammar, but we were never taught the most important subject of all—how to be successful. All the real life skills and principles that it takes to be successful are never taught in school. They are learned the hard way through trial and error, through failing in relationships, through failing in business, and through depression and desperation. The journey to success can be long and difficult, which is why so many people simply give up on their dreams and goals.

I'm going to be showing you how to achieve the success you desire, without the heartache and without years and years of struggle. You see, what I've discovered is that success in life doesn't have to be hard at all. The reality is, success is *simple*, but only *if* you know the formula.

The one key factor that all successful people have is nothing more than belief. Belief in themselves, belief that they can achieve their dreams, belief that they have everything they need right now to get started toward the lifestyle they desire.

The major difference between successful people and the average person is that successful people believe in themselves, their abilities, and their faith so strongly that they know without a doubt that they'll achieve their goals. It's this mind-set that will single you out for success.

It's Easier Than You Think

Not only must you believe changing your life is possible, but you must also believe that it can be easier than you think. Let me explain.

Have you ever been around someone who *always* has a reason why things are difficult? When you ask this kind of person how he or she is doing, the response might be, "Oh, I'm getting by." The sad truth is that most people have a mind-set that life is *hard*. Success is *hard*. Losing weight is *hard*. Earning a million dollars is *hard*.

I'm sure *you're* not like this, but maybe you know someone who is. ☺

Here's a secret. Ask Donald Trump how easy it is for him to earn a million dollars and what do you think he would tell you? Pretty obvious, right? He'd tell you it's the easiest thing in the world.

You'd probably agree with me if I said that the average person believes it is extremely difficult to earn over $100,000 a year. But if you were to ask any number of million-dollar business owners how easy it would be for them to earn six-figures, I guarantee you they'll tell you it's easy. It may be hard work, but they have absolute certainty. These business owners have no question whatsoever in the fact that they'll be successful. They have total faith!

At this point, you may be saying the reason they think it's easy is because these people are good at whatever it is they do. But what I want to propose is the exact opposite.

The reason successful people are good is not because they're just good, but because they *believe* they're good. They have *faith* that they're going to be successful. That belief and faith creates the mind-set that it truly *is* easy for them to be a success.

Here's where my life started taking a radical shift toward success: When I started intensely studying successful people, I realized that there was something different about them. They never talked about how success was *hard* to come by. They would talk about hard work, but their mind-set wasn't that it was hard. Their mind-set was that it was *certain*. Everything about them projected faith, belief, and certainty. Everything about them projected confidence in their abilities.

So that's where I adopted the concept of *easy*.

If you want to have a perfect example of this mental strategy in action, watch the movie *Wag the Dog*.

In this film, Dustin Hoffman plays a Hollywood movie producer who gets hired by the government to "manufacture" a war and get the American people distracted from something the president has done. If you watch the movie, you'll see that Dustin Hoffman keeps running into devastating problems. Yet each time disaster strikes, Dustin Hoffman's attitude is, "No problem! This is *easy!*" No matter what happens, he is absolutely and totally confident that they can pull it off—and guess what—they do!

In this movie, Dustin Hoffman is the perfect example of the principle of *easy* in action.

Controlling Your Mind

The moment I started shifting my mind-set, I started controlling my thoughts instead of letting my thoughts control me. Whenever a negative thought crept in, like "It's so *hard*," I would consciously repeat that thought to myself but say the exact opposite: "It's so *easy.*" I started controlling my speech to eliminate any words and statements that didn't fit this *easy* philosophy.

I'm going to get deep into the science of the mind behind this strategy in a moment, but before I do I want to give you a warning.

Please don't confuse this with the Law of Attraction, where people say, "All you have to do is *think* about what you want and it will *come* to you." That sounds great and sheep buy into it because they're sheep. Let's be clear on this, nothing is going to *come* to you. You have to go out and *get* it. You have to work your tail off in many cases. You have to chase your dreams down with fire and passion. So I'm not at all saying, "Don't work hard." In fact, I'm saying the opposite. I'm saying you should go after what you want in life with everything you've got.

On the flip side, there are plenty of people who work extremely hard and never get anywhere. Success is really as simple as one formula:

The ONE and ONLY formula for success:
SUCCESS = Your Skill × Your Effort
(Your success is equal to your level of skill multiplied by your level of effort.)

The *easy* principle is a huge multiplier for your level of skill because when your mind believes something is easy, it actually becomes easier for you.

When you have a mind-set that something is easy for you, you have less stress and more confidence. Confidence, which we'll talk more about in Chapter 7, is a huge multiplier in your success. The more confident you are, the more you'll likely put forth maximum effort and the more success you'll achieve.

At this point, you may have one giant question: How do you develop the mind-set that it's all *easy?*

I've heard trainers say it's as simple as just eliminating any negative thoughts, eliminating any negative words, and flipping a switch. Just believe it's easy for you because your mind has the ability to believe whatever you tell it to.

That sure sounds "easy," doesn't it? And it is for some people who can simply understand this principle, flip a switch in their

Adopt the "Easy" Principle.

mind, and poof, they have it. There is definitely some truth to that; we make things harder than they really are, so what I'm definitely encouraging is to use the *easy* principle—to *adopt* the *easy* principle.

For me, it wasn't exactly that simple.

When I entered into my first entrepreneurial venture, I was a broke college student, drowning in debt and working for minimum wage. My vision of where I saw myself at the time, or my identity, was that of a broke college student who had been poor most of his life. I was constantly talking about how much money I didn't have and how broke I was. What happened was that no matter how many goals I created for myself, my true identity, which is really controlled by your subconscious mind, was trained to be broke.

I remember turning 21 years old and, because I was working incredibly hard, I started earning a really strong income of as much as $2,000 a week. It was a totally new experience for me and completely outside of my belief that I was this broke kid who was in a constant state of struggle. I started going out all the time, partying, putting money in ridiculous investments, making stupid business decisions, and essentially self-sabotaging myself. What happened was that within a few short months, I was back to being broke and even farther in debt than ever.

You see, one of the most powerful driving forces in anyone's life is the identity that he or she has created.

My identity was that I was an ambitious, hardworking, broke kid who was always struggling to make it. Some people have an identity of being late all the time, an identity of being overweight, an identity of being a bad communicator, lousy in business, undisciplined, or any number of beliefs about themselves that hold them back in life.

I'm here to tell you that whatever limiting beliefs you've created for yourself are absolute and total crap and are nothing more than a story you've made up about yourself. What I want you to realize is that you *are* in control of creating whatever empowering or disempowering identity you've made up.

I'm not saying you have to change your positive beliefs or certainly any religious beliefs. What I'm saying is that you have the power to keep the beliefs that empower you and make you a better person, *and* you have the ability to change the beliefs that hold you back and limit the amount of success and personal fulfillment you experience.

Your thoughts literally control the amount of success you'll achieve.

The Three Ways to Develop a Belief

Look at the middle three letters of the word "beliefs" and you'll see L-I-E—lie. What I suggest you accept is that any disempowering belief you have about yourself is nothing more than a lie. It may be an opinion, but it's never a fact.

Just think, your beliefs (your lies) are what have shaped exactly who you are today. I'm not saying to change anything you love about yourself. What I want you to change are the negative beliefs, whether it's a lack of self-confidence, low self-esteem, feelings of hopelessness, challenges in relationships, being overweight, or anything else that you want to improve and conquer once and for all so you can live the life you were meant to live.

If your beliefs—which shape your personal identity—determine your success, then the big question is: How do you change them to create the results you want?

First you need to know the three ways you create a belief:

- Your experiences
- What other people have said about you (your outside programming)
- What you think and say about yourself (your internal programming)

Experiences Shape Our Beliefs

Every experience you've been through in life has been forever deposited somewhere in your subconscious mind. Those deposits were the first major factor that gave you the foundation of your identity.

What is more important than that realization is recognizing they have absolutely no relevance on your future success. If you've failed in the past, you can adopt the belief that you're a failure. That's the common process people go through, which is a major reason most people never reach anywhere close to their potential.

What separates those who fulfill that potential from those who don't has nothing to do with past failures. In fact, in most cases, the most successful people in the world actually have *more* failures than the rest.

A powerful way to look at past experiences is adopting a mind-set and belief that with every failure, you are now one step closer to success.

Tom Watson, the founder of IBM, once said that if you want to greatly increase your chance of success, double your rate of failure. When you ask most multimillionaires what their secret to success is, many of them will tell you that it's simply that they've learned what *not* to do through failing multiple times.

I've heard lots of people talk about celebrating successes, and I agree. No matter how small your successes are, you should celebrate them. The distinction, which will separate you from the masses, is that I also want you to start celebrating your failures. More specifically, you should celebrate your failures *as* successes.

Rather than whine, complain, and get depressed when things go wrong, *get excited* and use those as learning and character-building exercises.

One of the most powerful examples of putting this concept into practice for me came when I started my first Internet marketing company. I launched a company with a friend of mine who I had known for many years and we experienced some pretty phenomenal success right out of the gates. Within just a matter of months, we were generating over $100,000 per month and growing. Life was great and it seemed like we had the world in the palm of our hands.

Unfortunately, this was a new experience for both my partner and me. This was more success than either one of us had ever experienced, so we were taking massive profits out on a weekly basis. I was responsible for sales and marketing and my partner handled the operations and the money side of the business.

One day I got a call from one of our vendors asking why he hadn't been paid in the last month. Since I didn't handle the money, I had no idea and was totally confused. I went to my business partner and quickly found out that we were actually spending more money than we were earning and we were in debt about $10,000.

This is the moment when I knew philosophically that I had a very different opinion as to how business should be conducted than my partner did. I said that we absolutely needed to *stop* paying ourselves until we had paid off the debt. He had the belief that we were the most important people in the equation and that *we* had to be paid *first*, before our vendors.

You can imagine my dilemma, realizing that I had been in partnership with someone with an attitude that I believed would completely ruin our business reputation. After some heated arguments, he agreed and I thought all would be fine. I was scheduled to travel to Egypt for 10 days and when I returned, our Director of Operations called me up and said, "Matt, we need to talk."

He walked me through the bank records and showed me that the very day I left, my business partner, who had agreed to pay off our debt before paying anything to ourselves, took out over $2,000. Then just a few days later, he did the exact same thing again!

I was furious! But it didn't stop there. We started looking into our bank records from the previous months and discovered that he had not only been using company funds to pay for his personal expenses to the tune of thousands of dollars, but we were in debt much more than the $10,000. I can't even begin to tell you how foolish and stupid I felt for not taking responsibility for understanding the financial side of the business, trusting someone else to do it, and allowing this to happen.

That was a pivotal moment in my business career—I had the choice to either give up and tell myself I just wasn't cut out for business, or to celebrate the experience and use it as a lesson to become a strong leader in business.

I'll be honest—it took some serious soul-searching and lots of prayer, but what I decided to do was to simply celebrate the experience, thank God for the challenge He was putting me through, and ask for His strength to give me the courage, leadership, and tenacity to turn it around.

I could have decided to let this failure build upon my identity as a bad and inexperienced businessman, or choose to have this failure build upon my identity as a strong leader, as someone who can handle any challenge that arises and end up being more successful than ever before. I chose the latter.

Because I chose which belief about myself to accept, I didn't give up. I ended my partnership and took over the business. Within a few months I paid off tens of thousands of dollars of debt without having to file bankruptcy.

You see, no matter what the universe throws your way, you have the choice to take those experiences as reasons to build a weak personal identity or a strong personal identity. Which way do you think will get you closer to your dreams?

What People Say Shapes Our Beliefs

The second way we shape our beliefs is by listening to what other people say about us.

A perfect example of this goes back to something my mother said when I was about 11 years old. Now before I tell this story, I want to make it clear that my mom was, without a doubt, the greatest mother I could ever imagine. She was my role model growing up and is still my role model today. She has more integrity than anyone I've ever met and, despite the challenges we went through in my childhood, she went on to work her way through college, finish law school, and is now a judge.

So here's the story. I was in the sixth grade and living in Lubbock, Texas. We had just moved there from Dallas and I was in a new school. During our athletics class, we were told to run a one-mile race. Now I had never been overly athletic but was also not in bad shape by any means; just an average, skinny 11-year-old kid.

It took about six laps around the football field to equal one mile. After the first three laps, I was within the top 10 kids. Always pretty competitive, I turned it up a few notches and ran my heart out. I still remember feeling my heart pound so hard it felt like it was going to explode. As we crossed the finish line, I was about two steps behind the winner and I finished in second place. I was ecstatic! I remember racing home that day after school to tell Mom because I was so proud.

When I told her, she was so happy for me, gave me a big hug and said something to the effect of, "Wow, that's great because we're not good runners at all," referring to our family, who had never been any good at athletics. I remember thinking to myself almost immediately that what I did must have been a fluke because our family is bad at running.

That was the very last time in my childhood I came anywhere close to winning a race.

Looking back at that now, I can see that there was absolutely no basis for the fact that because our family had been bad at running that I somehow had to be bad at running, too. In fact, just the opposite was true based on my results of coming in second place. But because someone I loved and looked up to made one simple statement, I took on that statement as a belief for myself.

We obviously can't go back into the past and change what negative things we've heard, but we can realize that what someone says about you has no basis in reality unless you *choose* to believe it. From this point forward, make a commitment that you won't allow anyone in your life to say disempowering statements about you.

When someone says anything about me that is contrary to the person I want to become, whether it's that I don't have the experience or that I can't do something, I simply say something to the effect of, "Please don't ever say that to me again." When you set those ground rules for people, you'll find that it does shock them, but because you're showing respect for yourself, they in turn naturally respect you more for setting that standard.

If someone continues to say disempowering things about you, you absolutely *must* separate yourself from him or her. If someone can't respect you, he or she doesn't deserve having you in their presence. Spend time with people who celebrate you, not belittle you.

What We Tell Ourselves Shapes Our Beliefs

The third and most important way you shape your beliefs is what you say and think about yourself—your internal programming.

Every word, action, and thought enters into your subconscious mind and produces either a negative or positive result. If you put something negative in, you will only get a negative result. If you put something positive in, you produce a positive result. Everything you put into your mind, every thought, every word, and every action gets registered into your subconscious, and those deposits actually create who you are.

Your subconscious mind completely controls your success because it's infinitely more powerful than your conscious mind. It believes and acts upon everything you tell it. So if you tell yourself you're broke, you're tired, and you hate your job, your subconscious mind figures out a way to create and enhance those results. If you tell yourself you're wealthy, you're energized, and you're happy, your subconscious begins doing everything in its power to create *that* reality.

The Power of Lies

Here's another trick. Your subconscious mind does not know the difference between a truth and a lie. It simply does its best to carry out exactly what you've programmed it to believe. So when you say, "I'm sexy, I'm confident, I'm a millionaire," your conscious mind may be telling you you're full of it, but your subconscious, which is much more powerful, takes that as a command and works out a way for you to be all of those things.

The key is constantly filling your subconscious mind with empowering, uplifting, and motivating deposits. If you profess what you don't want, you actually become *more* of that negative thought because you keep reinforcing that identity.

What you focus on expands.

The Law of Consistency

The most difficult thing in the world for people to change is their identity, because it's who they believe they are. There's an important law of human nature called consistency that states we have a natural urge and tendency to remain consistent with who we think we are.

When you've programmed your identity to be overweight, consciously you may want to get thin, but subconsciously you've programmed your mind to believe you're an overweight person. Because your subconscious mind is so much more powerful than your conscious mind, it does everything it can to keep you consistent with the identity of an overweight person.

If you've been on all kinds of diets, but nothing's worked, my suggestion is to look at the root cause as to *why* you're overweight. I can promise you that it's not that the "diet" didn't work. Losing weight is actually an incredibly simple formula; when you burn more calories than you consume, you lose weight. When you consume more calories than you burn, you gain weight. What keeps you overweight, more than anything else, is your mental process and identity about being overweight.

Sometimes people claim they just don't have the willpower to lose weight. By simply speaking the words, "I don't have the willpower," you make yourself believe it's true. Because you have an identity of being overweight, *of course* you're going to have these "irresistible" cravings because your subconscious mind constantly looks for ways to keep you overweight to maintain the identity you've created for yourself.

What you want to concentrate on is changing your vision and belief about yourself. Every time you start to think or say to yourself that you're fat, flip it and say, "I'm perfectly fit, healthy, and sexy." Please don't get discouraged. You've formed your identity over years and years of subconscious programming, so you may not be able to change any negative identity overnight. Focus on overriding any negative belief with a new positive belief and you'll gradually change into the healthy, positive person you truly want to become.

I'll share an internal programming example I created for myself on becoming wealthy. For most of my childhood, we grew up poor. Mom worked her way through school, often working two jobs, and many times we were on food stamps. I was the kid who had the free lunch pass at school. We lived in a trailer park one year and another year lived in a little one-room apartment above a garage. It was so small that when you sat on the toilet your knees touched the shower.

Even though we were broke, my mom worked her way through school to become an attorney. However, her starting salary was so low that she had to work two jobs just to take care of me. That taught me two important lessons.

First, it's important to work extremely hard to get what you want out of life. Second, no matter how hard you work, money is always hard to come by.

Because that's what I experienced, that's what I believed. So it was no surprise that when I became an entrepreneur at age 18, I had a ton of discipline and an intense work ethic. But no matter how hard I worked, I never had enough money. I kept getting further and further in debt and constantly told myself and other people how broke I was.

You see, every time I said, "I'm broke," I was programming my subconscious mind to create that identity. No matter how many goals I set to make money, what I truly expected for myself (my identity and belief about myself) was that I was always broke.

My subconscious cheerfully did everything in its power to keep me broke. Even when I started making some money, I would always end up losing it and staying in debt because I didn't believe I could be someone who was anything but broke.

What turned my life around was when I realized I had to change the identity I built for myself. When I started refusing to say that I was broke or in debt, or even to think about myself as anything but a complete and total success, my life started to change.

I started declaring to myself that I was wealthy and that money was easy to come by. I started declaring what I wanted, not what I was currently experiencing. Before you can reach your goals, you must first believe you are the type of person who can achieve them.

No more MEDIOCRITY.

I had to declare that I was a millionaire to myself before I could actually become one.

You don't gain confidence in yourself after you have success. You gain confidence in yourself before you ever achieve success. Belief and confidence come before the result of success. Belief is that leap of faith that takes you to where you really want to be.

So take a look at what you want to improve in your own life and then honestly look at how you've created your identity through your words, thoughts, and actions. To change, you must first become conscious of your disempowering words and thoughts and then flip them around to declare affirmatively what you want.

If you're late all the time, you've simply built that as your identity. If you're bad at time management and can't get anything done during the day, you've simply built into your identity that you're bad at time management. If you're a terrible public speaker, you've simply made that your identity. The good news is that everything you are right now is only because you believe it to be true.

Here's how to shift your life in a positive direction: First, *stop declaring anything negative about yourself to be true!* I hear people say, "There's just not enough time in the day." Guess what? Every time you say that, you make it *more* true for yourself. When you profess weakness, you become weak. When you profess cowardice, you become a coward. When you profess hatred, you get hatred.

Starting right now, start declaring wealth, start declaring health, start declaring happiness, start declaring love, start declaring everything you want for your life and you'll start to build an identity that allows you to become the person you want to be.

Don't wallow in mediocrity one second longer than necessary. The reason average people are average is because they walk around their entire lives being miserable, saying things like, "If I can just find the right man or woman, then I'll be happy." Unfortunately, life doesn't work that way.

Whatever you want to attract, you have to become that type of person before you will get any results. Your dream spouse is probably someone who wants to be with someone who's *already* happy and excited about life. Until you become the kind of person who will attract him or her, you will never have that person. Remember, you can never *have* and then *be*; you must *be* and then you will *have*.

> *Watch your thoughts, they become your words. Watch your words, they become your actions. Watch your actions, they become your habits. Watch your habits, they become your character. Watch your character for it will become your destiny.*

—Frank Outlaw

4

Impotent Dreams Produce
Impotent Results

*You will never live life beyond your wildest
expectations until you first have some wild
expectations.*

—Author Unknown

In one episode of the classic TV show *The Twilight Zone*, an elderly couple rubs an old lamp and discovers a genie inside, who offers to grant the couple four wishes. Thinking the genie is a fraud, the couple immediately wishes to fix a broken pane of glass. Puzzled, the genie asks, "That's it? That's *all* you really wish for?"

When the elderly couple insist that's all they wish for, the genie laughs and fixes the broken glass with the wave of his hand. Immediately after seeing this, the elderly couple start arguing, accusing the other of wasting a wish on such a trivial matter.

While this fictional couple eventually learns about the power of wishes, many people in the real world do not. Rather than wish for something tremendous and awe-inspiring, they settle for puny,

Dream big dreams.

trivial goals like fixing a broken pane of glass. When they get exactly what they wish for, they're still unhappy because, like that elderly couple, they wished for something that really makes no difference in their lives.

Although you don't have a genie to grant wishes, you have something better. Unlike a genie, who can only make a handful of your dreams come true, you have the power to make *all* of your dreams come true. As soon as you come up with another dream, you have the power to make that one come true as well. But until you first identify a dream, all the wishes in the world will get you nowhere, especially if you wish for something so miniscule that it won't improve your life one bit. That's why I can't overemphasize the importance of having a powerful dream.

Dreams Are the Fuel That Fire Desire

In his book *All You Can Do Is All You Can Do*, Art Williams said that once you've rooted your desire so firmly in your mind that you think about it all the time, your desire becomes a commitment. When you make a commitment, you've got to burn all your bridges, so retreat simply isn't an option.

Desire is the one element that keeps you going when things get rough. It's what separates the losers who give up from the winners who do whatever it takes to reach their dreams.

Former football coach Vince Lombardi said it best with his famous quote: "Winning isn't everything, but wanting to win is."

Every great athlete I've ever met has this insatiable desire to win. It's something deep down in his or her gut that burns within. Think back to when you had such a huge desire for something that you could barely sleep at night.

One of the secret characteristics of successful people is that they just want it so bad they can't stand it. Because of that desire, they make it happen. They figure out how to be successful because success is burning within them. When their head tells them they *can't*, something deep inside tells them that they *must*.

You can have a great education, but you won't win without desire.

You can have a ton of talent, but you won't win without desire.

You can have a ton of experience, but you still won't win without desire.

Desire is the secret.

So if desire is the secret to winning, what's the secret to desire? *Dreams* are the fuel that fire desire.

Dreams give you the motivation to get back on your feet when you're knocked down. Dreams are what give you the belief in yourself that lets you say to yourself, "I can, I will, and I must."

Believe that every man, woman, and child are created equal. If one person can achieve his or her dreams, that means you can achieve your dreams as well. If you don't pursue your dreams, part of you dies inside.

Dreams give you energy, life, and fulfillment. The most commonly accepted definition of success in the personal development world is the steady progression toward a worthwhile goal or *dream*.

Begin to imagine the most that's possible for your life. Remember, no matter what your current level of thinking might be, you're probably dreaming too small. Dream big dreams that inspire you. If your dream doesn't scare you, it's probably not big enough.

I know you wouldn't be reading this book right now if you didn't have a great deal of desire, but I want you to know that the greater your desire burning within you, the greater level of success you'll ultimately achieve.

I've heard teachers, leaders, and business executives say things like, "Billy just doesn't have the desire." As if desire is a trait you're either born with or not.

Here's the reality. *Desire* is something that must be created and harnessed from within. We all have the same desire put in us at birth, so why is it that by the time we reach adulthood, some people have a ton of it and some people have very little? There's no such thing as a person with a low level of desire. There are only people who have impotent dreams!

If you want to harness your passion, your drive, your discipline, and your determination, you have to have a burning desire. The formula for creating that desire is through dreams. To make a radical shift in your level of success, make a radical shift to break out of the common thinking that you've been trapped in. Begin to dream about the huge possibilities that are available for your life.

I am married to what I consider the most beautiful woman on earth. She has the most amazing heart, the most amazing mind and soul of any woman that I've ever met. One of the reasons we're both so attracted to each other is because we both love to dream big dreams. In fact, it's one of our favorite hobbies.

Many nights we'll sit on the couch and talk about where we'll be in five years. How we'll be able to take our private jet, load it down with supplies to Third World countries, and make an impact on people's lives who can't help themselves. We dream about how we'll be responsible for saving the lives of thousands upon thousands of children who are dying because of starvation. We'll sit and dream together about helping create financial freedom for thousands of other people. How we'll rent out entire cruise ships filled with people we've helped achieve success. How we'll take vacations with our friends to places that most people only dream about. How we'll educate our children and teach them history by going to the places in the world that most children only read about in books.

Realize that there are *millions* of millionaires around the world. So if it's possible to reach that level, why accept anything less?

For years, I used to get caught up feeling guilty about dreaming big dreams that seemed overly materialistic. But when Warren Buffett donated billions of dollars to the Bill and Melinda Gates Foundation, I realized that there's an abundance of wealth to be shared. So instead of thinking lack and scarcity, I began to realize that I could have material possessions, just like Mr. Buffett, *and* make a huge contribution to society. In fact, the material things themselves have little meaning. What really has meaning is the person you have to become and the difference you make in the lives of others in order to create that type of wealth.

Write Your Obituary Before You're Dead

One way to plan your life is by thinking about what your obituary will say when you pass away. Here's a powerful story about a gentleman named Alfred from Stockholm, Sweden.

Although Alfred was tutored at home, he was mostly self-educated. He was an avid reader of literature and became fluent in several languages including English, French, German, Russian, and Swedish. More importantly, he also became a chemist.

Alfred soon began experimenting with nitroglycerine and received a Swedish patent for a detonator dubbed the "Nobel Lighter." He soon set up a factory near Stockholm to manufacture nitroglycerine. Unfortunately, nitroglycerine is dangerous to handle and Alfred's factory blew up in 1864, killing Alfred's younger brother, Emil.

The explosion did not slow Alfred down, however. Within just a month, he organized other factories to manufacture nitroglycerine. Three years later, Alfred combined nitroglycerine with an inert substance that made the explosive safer to handle and store. This new, safer explosive was Alfred's invention, which he called dynamite.

Despite being a pacifist, Alfred saw his invention used for war. In 1888, Alfred's brother Ludvig died in France. When Alfred read the obituary in a French newspaper, his grief turned to dismay. Instead of reading his brother's obituary, he found that he was reading his own obituary, which the newspaper had mistakenly printed!

"The Merchant of Death Is Dead!" the headline proclaimed. Upon further reading, Alfred found that his obituary described him as a man who had simply gotten rich by making it easier for people to kill each other.

Dismayed by what he had read, Alfred vowed that his real obituary would be far different than what the French newspaper had printed. Instead of being a man who had become wealthy from the misery and suffering of others, Alfred decided his obituary would portray him as a man of peace who had used his wealth to benefit humanity.

(continued)

When he died eight years later in 1896, Alfred had left more than $9,000,000 to fund awards for work that helped promote peace. You probably know Alfred best from the awards that are still given out today in his honor. They're called Nobel Peace Prizes in honor of Mr. Alfred Nobel.

Now the question you have to ask yourself is this: How do you want to be remembered? Right now, you have the power to shape your own destiny and write your future obituary. What will it say? Only you can decide how you want your life to turn out.

Success Breeds Success

The more success you have, the more you'll believe you can achieve. Until you start succeeding, you'll have nothing but your own desire to power you toward your goal. Keeping that white hot fuel of desire burning by yourself can be difficult, so surround yourself with successful people, even if they aren't chasing after the same goals that you are.

Simply being around and listening to successful people keeps you excited about your own dreams. When you surround yourself with other people who are overflowing with desire and a passion in life to succeed, you can't help but get some of that desire on you as well.

Not only do I want you to start surrounding yourself with people who have desire and motivation to change their life, I want you to immerse yourself by listening to successful people every day. When you hear personal development speakers with a ton of desire, you can't help but pick up part of that desire to reach your own dreams as well.

What's helped drive me to an insane level of desire and success is to turn my car into "Drive-Time University." When I'm traveling, I'm constantly listening to success and motivation CDs that uplift me and raise my level of desire. Here's what I know as a fact—no singer, no band, no music is going to build me into a success. My success and my family's success and the legacy that I'll leave when I'm gone is infinitely more important than listening to talk shows or music on the radio.

The average person spends approximately an hour a day in their vehicle. If you spent five days a week listening to personal development programs instead of the radio, you would give yourself over 250 hours of empowerment every year!

I've probably listened to thousands of hours of content because I've been doing this for years. I've listened to some of the programs over 10 times because I know that repetition is the mother of all skill. That one strategy of turning your vehicle into "Drive-Time University" will make a major difference in your life.

Don't Be a "Try-Baby"

If you want to achieve any goal, your first step is to declare it. Take 100 percent responsibility for creating it and then clear out all the words like "hopefully," "can't," "maybe"—and the killer, "try."

When someone tells me they're going to "try" to do something, I always know they're *not* going to do it. "Try" is nothing more than a front-end excuse when you have no commitment. Words like "try" are signs that you have no faith and you're using your own power against yourself.

Never allow yourself to become a "try-baby."

You see, when we were children, we had an amazing ability to dream. Think about this for a minute. When children are asked what they're going to be when they grow up, what do they say? Do they say, "I'm going to *try* to be millionaire"? Do they say, "I'm going to *try* to be an astronaut"? Do they say, "I'm going to *try* to be a professional athlete"? No. They have their dream, and that's what they're going to be. Period.

Children know the power of dreaming big because they want to live a big life. Unfortunately, though, what happens to most kids is that they grow up and start hearing their parents or teachers telling them to be realistic. The adults of the world tell them to "get their head out of the clouds."

When children hear this from enough people, they begin to doubt their own dreams and themselves. Eventually, they end up lowering their dreams and aspirations to adapt to society's "norms," which essentially means they let society steal their dreams.

By the time most of us become adults, we've lost that childlike enthusiasm for life. Instead of having goals like owning their own multimillion-dollar home, too many people settle for goals like just getting out of debt. Instead of dreaming about earning millions of dollars from their investments, adults embrace goals like just having enough money to pay all their bills. Because they lack a dream, the average person is content with living a life of mediocrity.

When kids are around six years old, they see their parents as their heroes. Then around the age of sixteen, most kids look at their parents and wonder, "What happened?" Their parents have gone from grown-ups to given-ups. Unfortunately, these same kids usually follow in the footsteps of their parents and give up on their dreams as well.

Instead of dreaming big, they settle for lesser dreams they feel more comfortable in going after. Instead of dreaming about having the financial freedom to live anywhere they want in the world, they dream about making their rent for the next month.

Instead of dreaming big and picking a goal that would give them more time to spend with their family and loved ones, they dream about spending two measly weeks out of every year on vacation.

You need to dream big because, believe it or not, it takes just a little more effort to achieve a big dream than it does to achieve a small one.

It's a fact of life that people tend to mimic what they see around them. If you surround yourself with successful people, then you'll want to fit in and be successful, too. If you surround yourself with negative people and pessimistic news, guess what? There's a good chance you'll forget about your big dreams, accept the small dreams that society says are more realistic, and go through the rest of your life in a rut wondering what went wrong. The next time you feel like you're in a rut, just remember that the only difference between a rut and a grave is the depth of the hole.

Most men die at age 25 and are buried at 65.

—Dr. Nicolas M. Butler

Creating Your Lifetime Dream List

I'm going to share something I've been doing for years that I know, beyond a shadow of a doubt, has helped me achieve success. If you are truly serious about achieving your dreams, it's an exercise that I encourage you to complete immediately.

Create a "Dream List" of at least 100 things you want to do while you're still alive. I first created my list when I was 24 years old and it still sits at the very front of my planner that I use every day.

I'll give you an example of the first 10 items I put on my list when I was 24 years old:

1. Dodge Viper
2. 150 foot yacht with a helicopter landing pad, satellite communication systems, wave runners, and a ski boat
3. Lamborghini
4. Gulfstream Jet
5. Mountain home in Colorado with hot tub overlooking mountains, heated floors, glass walls on the side looking down the mountain, private lake on 15,000 acres of land
6. 15,000-square-foot home in the city with marble floors, dual staircases upon entry, three floors with theater that seats 50 people
7. Private secluded island with port for my yacht
8. Travel to 150 countries
9. Have close personal friends on every continent
10. Become the founder of a charitable organization donating millions per year to charity

When I look back at my entire list, which I'm still building today, it's amazing how many of those dreams I've actually accomplished. I've vacationed in Australia, cruised down the Nile River, gotten scuba certified and went scuba diving with the sharks in Bora Bora, skydived, learned to surf, vacationed to Hawaii, learned how to speed read, petted a stingray, relaxed on the beach in Tahiti, went to the top of the Eiffel Tower (where I proposed to my wife), went on an African safari, cruised the Mediterranean, went bungee jumping, had sushi in Japan, wrote a book and became a best-selling author, starred in a movie, took a vacation as an adult with just me and my mother, walked on fire, ate fire, rode in a hot air balloon, visited the Holy Lands, saw the Coliseum in Rome and the Leaning Tower of Pisa, and dozens of other experiences that have made my life amazing.

When I started this list, I couldn't even imagine some of these dreams as possible, but because I put them on paper, I took the first step to turning those dreams into reality. If it wasn't for making those dreams real, I know that I never would have accomplished even half of what I've been able to do so far.

Now it's time to turn on *your* dream machine. Remember that no matter what your current level of thinking is, you're probably thinking too small. Create a dream list that inspires you—dreams that are more than you can even imagine possible.

Right now, I want you to start creating your dream list. Keep going until you have at least 100 dreams written down!

1. Become an Internet Entrepreneur
2. Travel all over the world
3. Read a lot of history
4. Learn new languages
5. Take up Art as a hobby
6. Become an author
7. Clean up all clutter
8. Start a comic book series
9. Blogging on certain interests
10. Have close friendships
11. Promote Goa as a destination
12. Watch all good movies
13. Give up petty novels
14. Start a charitable organization
15. Maintain my car
16. Buy a big house
17. Get a new car
18. Sponsor and promote
19. Have vacation homes
20. Find the woman of my dreams
21. Connect with my old friends
22.
23.
24.
25.
26.
27.
28.
29.
30.
31.
32.
33.
34.

35 _____	68 _____
36 _____	69 _____
37 _____	70 _____
38 _____	71 _____
39 _____	72 _____
40 _____	73 _____
41 _____	74 _____
42 _____	75 _____
43 _____	76 _____
44 _____	77 _____
45 _____	78 _____
46 _____	79 _____
47 _____	80 _____
48 _____	81 _____
49 _____	82 _____
50 _____	83 _____
51 _____	84 _____
52 _____	85 _____
53 _____	86 _____
54 _____	87 _____
55 _____	88 _____
56 _____	89 _____
57 _____	90 _____
58 _____	91 _____
59 _____	92 _____
60 _____	93 _____
61 _____	94 _____
62 _____	95 _____
63 _____	96 _____
64 _____	97 _____
65 _____	98 _____
66 _____	99 _____
67 _____	100 _____

5

Goal Setting Is for Losers

If you don't know where you are going,
any road will get you there.

—Lewis Carroll

The personal development industry may cast me away forever
for the title of this chapter. After all, if you go back to the
first personal development books ever written, you'll find endless
advice on the power of goal setting, and the same is true for most
personal development books written today.

However, if you're like me, you've probably set goal after goal
with grand ambitions—only to fall short time after time, leaving
you frustrated to the point where you feel like giving up on goal
setting altogether.

So am I saying don't set goals? Actually, not at all.

The overall process is sound advice. I definitely believe in
the old saying, "Dreams keep you going, but your goals keep you
on track." I do, however, also believe that the typical goal setting
process needs some fine-tuning.

Here's the issue: When you study subconscious programming as I touched on earlier, you'll remember that every word and every thought is a deposit into your subconscious mind.

Again, your subconscious mind is infinitely more powerful than your conscious mind. When your subconscious believes something to be true, based on what you have told it though your thoughts and words, it does everything in its power to create that identity.

Example: Just like we mentioned in Chapter 3 on beliefs, an overweight person who says he or she is fat all the time is programming his or her subconscious mind. As the subconscious gets programmed through those words, the core identity of the person becomes that of a fat person. When your core identity is being fat, your subconscious mind creates irresistible cravings, the urge to overeat, lack of motivation to exercise, and so forth, to match the subconscious mind's programming.

This is the exact problem with "goal" setting.

The word "goal" itself is something you do *not* yet have.

So when you tell yourself, "My goal is to be a millionaire" that presupposes in your subconscious mind that you are *not* a millionaire. Each time you say, "My goal is to be a millionaire" you are essentially programming your subconscious that you are exactly the opposite, that you are *not* a millionaire. As you program yourself over and over, your identity is created as the person who does *not* have what you desire. In turn, your subconscious does whatever it can to remain consistent with the negative identity that you've created through your "goal setting."

So the intention of goal setting is a noble one, but as the famous quote says, *"The road to hell is paved with good intentions."*

That's why I say that goal setting is for losers because if you follow the principles of traditional goal setting, you lock your subconscious mind into thinking of what you don't have. To be effective, you must state your goals in the present as if they're already true, which will program the subconscious mind to find a way to turn your goals into reality.

It's great to have dreams and goals and it's crucial to believe that you have everything in your power to achieve them. Now you

The subconscious does not know the difference between a truth and a lie

need the next step, which is a specific game plan to help you achieve those dreams.

In this chapter, I'm going to share a specific goal-setting formula that I've used for the past several years. Based on the dramatic increase in results in my life and in the lives of those I've mentored, I can promise you that if you follow this formula your life can improve dramatically within the next year. Think of goal setting like a game plan that gives specific directions and steps to take toward achieving a specific result.

The key characteristics for achieving any goal are:

1. You must have a specific goal.
2. You must have a specific time frame to achieve your goal.
3. You must write your goal down.
4. You must determine a compelling purpose why you must achieve your goal.
5. You must develop an action plan to reach your goal.
6. You must think about and look at your goal every day.

On the first few pages of my planner, I have a goals section that I review every day (see Table 5.1 for an example). Each page has a separate goal split up into three sections:

- Section 1 lists a specific goal with a deadline.
- Section 2 lists the reason why it's an absolute must to achieve that goal.
- Section 3 lists a specific action plan for achieving that goal.

Creating Specific Goals

Let's talk about Section 1 first. I cannot emphasize enough that you must be very specific about your goal. If you want to earn a full-time income, don't just write, "I'll be earning a full-time income by February 2." Instead write, "I *am* earning $100,000.00 per year by December 2 of next year through my business."

TABLE 5.1   Sample Goal-Setting Sheet

Goal and Deadline

To achieve the CAPM certification by May 2014

Purpose for Achieving Goal

To improve my chances on the job;

Action Plan for Achieving Goal

Enroll for Project Management course through LAPL, sign up with PMI, download PMBOK

Every time you read your goal, you'll be imprinting that specific goal and dollar figure into your subconscious mind.

Not only are you imprinting the goal into your subconscious, you're also imprinting that you *are* earning $100,000 per year. Typical goal setting has you look and sometimes even repeat out loud that you "will be" earning, which imprints into your subconscious that you "are not" earning it now. This slight shift in self-programming allows your subconscious to program your identity as a person who already has the goal you desire.

I say this a lot because it's so true—your subconscious does not know the difference between a truth and a lie. It simply acts upon what you tell it.

The subconscious mind is the part of your brain that brings out the motivation, the ability, and the creativity needed to accomplish your goal. Your subconscious doesn't interpret or assume what your conscious mind knows to be true. So if you are vague with your goals, your results will also be vague. For all your subconscious knows, a vague goal of earning a full-time income could be a full-time income at the poverty level in your existing job. If you want specific results, you must create specific goals.

Finding the Motivation behind a Specific Goal—Your Purpose

Section 2 must state the reason for your goal—your true motivation and purpose behind it. Having a goal of earning a full-time income is great, but to harness your true motivation, you must have a purpose that burns inside of you.

Let's take the goal of earning $100,000 a year as your own boss working from home. That might be fairly exciting, but it's also easy to feel overwhelmed by it all and let it drift away through inaction. However, if you dig a little deeper and figure out exactly why you want that type of income, you'll experience an entirely new level of motivation.

Rather than just stating that you want to earn $100,000 a year, here's a more compelling reason:

I am achieving this because I refuse to miss out on seeing my children grow up by trading my life away for a job.

Isn't that a lot more motivating than just saying you want to earn $100,000 a year as your own boss? Here's another example of a burning motivation:

I am achieving this because I must be a mentor and role model to my children, so they will never live a life of poverty and mediocrity.

This example is much more motivating. When you create a why behind every goal that inspires you, you'll create the motivation necessary to accomplish it.

Creating the Action Plan toward a Specific Goal

Section 3 is where the rubber meets the road. This is where you spell out exactly what you're going to do to accomplish each goal.

Here's an example of a plan to achieve a certain goal for someone who wants to get in shape:

- I exercise a minimum of 30 minutes, four times a week at the gym.
- I drink at least two liters of water every day.
- I count my calories and always stay under my daily limit.
- I always leave at least some food on my plate at every meal.
- I weigh myself once a week and record my weight in a journal so I can see the progress that I'm making.

With a list of action steps laid out in front of you in black and white, you'll have a simple road map to follow that makes achieving your goal that much easier.

The next step in the goal-setting process is to look at your goal every day. This is why I have my goals at the very front of my day planner. Every time I open my planner, my goals smack me right in the face. I have a reminder of each goal, the driving force behind it, and the necessary steps I must follow to make that goal a reality.

By seeing your goals every day, stated in positive terms as if they were already true, your subconscious mind starts to guide you in the right direction. Every imprint made in your subconscious mind creates your identity. Your identity creates your belief system. And your belief system creates your results. So every time you read your list of goals, you're burning them into your identity. When your goals become your identity, your subconscious mind works overtime to help make that identity a reality.

Now I want you to put this book down and get to work on your goals. Set your goals in a few areas for your life and remember—success isn't just about money. True success comes from balancing every area of your life.

Personally, I have goals for different parts of my life.

- Business and finances
- Health and fitness
- Family and relationship

- Personal learning and growth
- Fun and personal fulfillment

So stop right now and get to work putting your goals down on paper (see Table 5.2, pages 60–62). Each time you write a goal down, you're one step closer to achieving it.

If you're like me, just the simple act of writing down goals gets you motivated to take action to accomplish them and excited about your future. When you can see your goals as real, believable, and achievable, your life takes on a whole new level of energy and motivation. It's that zest for life that will help you reach any goal you want, no matter how great the obstacles may be.

TABLE 5.2   My Goals

Goal 1

Goal and Deadline   *Apply for U.S. Citizenship.*
by 09/20/13.

Purpose for Achieving Goal

I am achieving this so I can prepare to travel the world.

Action Plan for Achieving Goal

Get the forms, fill them out, attend library workshops.

Goal 2

Goal and Deadline

Purpose for Achieving Goal

Action Plan for Achieving Goal

Goal 3

Goal and Deadline

Purpose for Achieving Goal

Action Plan for Achieving Goal

Goal 4

Goal and Deadline

(Continued)

Purpose for Achieving Goal

Action Plan for Achieving Goal

Goal 5

Goal and Deadline

Purpose for Achieving Goal

Action Plan for Achieving Goal

Action Management for Peak Performance

Being rich is having money; being wealthy is having time.

—Margaret Bonnano

One of the most important qualities of almost every millionaire I know is that he or she is laser-focused on time management. Personally, I always have a hard time with the term "time management" because in reality, you can't manage time. But you can manage *action*. So what this chapter is all about is helping you master the art and science of action management.

I've spent thousands of dollars on different programs and seminars looking for the one perfect time management system. Unfortunately, that perfect system doesn't seem to exist. But by taking pieces from each one and some of my own, I came up with what I believe is as close to perfect as possible.

What I'll be sharing here is the exact action management system I use on a daily basis to keep myself laser focused on producing results while maximizing my free time so I can enjoy it with my family. You see, I believe wholeheartedly that because I manage my actions so well, I can get done in three hours what the average person does in eight. The key to being an Unemployed Millionaire is producing massive results while also having tremendous levels of free time to do what you love. There is absolutely no reason you can't have both!

Here's the first golden nugget of advice involving time management. Stop telling yourself, "There's just not enough *time* in the day." Every time you utter that statement, you strengthen your identity as someone who doesn't have enough time. The more you say things like that, the more you make them real and end up stuck in this vicious cycle of lack and scarcity. Bottom line—that statement is weak and every time you say it, you make yourself even weaker.

That may sound harsh, but it's that harshness that I had to use with myself. You see, that seemed to be my daily mantra. Every time I said there's not enough time in the day, I was shifting blame to something other than myself. I always had an excuse if I didn't get everything done. After all, it wasn't my fault! It was the fault of *time*.

Here's how I turned it around. Every time I started to think or say to myself, "There's just not enough time in the day," I'd turn it around and tell myself, "There's *more* than enough time in the day."

I had to change my internal programming as it related to time. I had to reprogram my subconscious to believe that I had plenty of time to get everything done. When I changed my programming, I made a quantum leap in my ability to produce.

Now don't get me wrong. Are there days when I don't get everything done I want to do? Of course. But by shifting my internal beliefs about time, I now stand from a place of power instead of a place of weakness.

The first step is taking responsibility for the fact that there is *plenty* of time every day to do what you want to do. We all have the same number of hours in a day.

Time is not the enemy, your belief about it is.

Unconscious Ego Management

Before I get into the details and how-tos of action management, let's address one of the overriding reasons why so many business-people are completely out of balance.

This may sound strange, but for many people, their overriding personal values *require* them to be a workaholic, stressed out, and out of balance. Consciously, they may say to themselves and others that they want more free time, but they'll never achieve it because it doesn't support their stronger personal values. Deep down, they actually *want* and *need* the stress.

I can hear it now: "Matt, you've been okay up until this point, but now I think you've gone off the deep end." Let me explain.

Here's the game I was running. I would work seven days a week, 80 to 100 hours, oftentimes sleeping in my office because I had *so* much to do. Many nights I would drive home at 2:00 in the morning completely exhausted and dead tired. But even though I could hardly see straight, I would have this huge sense of accomplishment for being such a hard worker.

The one word that really explains it all is *significance*.

One of the reasons we're driven to do what we do in life is based on our core values. At that time, even though I didn't realize it, my highest personal value was significance.

By being a workaholic, everyone talked about how hard I worked, how much discipline I had, and how they worried that I was working too much. All of which completely fed my ego and garnered enormous levels of significance.

I was always stressed out about my business and how much responsibility I had on my shoulders. No matter how much stress I had, I always seemed willing to take on more responsibilities because the stress fed my need for significance. My brain was wired to believe that high stress equaled important businessman. And important businessman equaled massive levels of significance.

Even though my body was breaking down, I was tired all the time, and approaching burnout, I was addicted to the feeding of my ego.

I essentially "got off" on the pain.

It wasn't until I was completely burned out that I finally opened my mind to the possibility that there could be a different way . . . that I might actually be able to get happiness not just from working hard, but by actually enjoying my life.

Once I finally stopped looking at my life from the inside out, the reason for my pathos became patently obvious.

Watching Yourself in a Movie

Being able to identify what drove my actions came from the ability to identify the "me" I was living versus the "real me."

I believe we all have two versions of our self. There is your ego, what I'm calling "me," and then there is the real you. Most people live their lives being controlled by their ego, never realizing that there is the real self, or their higher self. The higher self is infinitely more powerful in controlling your thoughts, feelings, and actions.

The real you can watch as if seeing yourself in a movie. When you put yourself in your higher self, you're able to watch yourself and separate the true self from what your ego is feeling. The real you looks at your ego and says: "There I am being hateful"; "There I am being depressed"; or "There I am feeling completely overjoyed."

Once I realized that a higher self existed within, I was able to look at the way I lived and say, "There I am working like a madman and making myself miserable because I'm looking for other people's validation to make me feel important."

The moment I separated myself from my ego and realized what truly drove my actions was the moment when I finally had the power to make a shift.

Once I identified that desire for significance was my primary driver, I decided to make a radical shift in my core values. I made a list of the values that were driving my behavior based on the way I was living. My list looked something like the following.

Primary Values:
1. Significance
2. Achievement

3. Confidence
4. Discipline
5. Integrity
6. Learning

Looking at my primary values, it was no wonder I was so completely out of balance.

The next step was identifying what primary values I was committed to adopting since I knew they are the dominant driver behind why we do what we do.

I decided to make a new list that looked like this.

1. Happiness
2. Love
3. Health and vitality
4. Integrity
5. Playfulness and fun
6. Passion
7. Achievement
8. Adventure
9. Growth and learning
10. Confidence

With my new set of primary values, I'd like to say that my actions completely shifted overnight. But the reality was that they shifted a little right away, and a little more and more over time.

The key is staying committed and focused on your primary values. To keep myself clear on the purpose behind my actions, I keep this list of primary values in my planner to refresh my memory often.

It's a simple sheet of paper that says:

I Constantly Move Toward:
1. Happiness
2. Love
3. Health and vitality
4. Etc.

If it hadn't been for this realization of the ego self versus higher self and the consequent values shifting process, I would most likely still be in the same "work myself to death" routine just so I could feel significant.

Based on that shift, I experience infinitely more joy because I'm fulfilled not by significance, but by the values I *choose* to live by.

The Unemployed Millionaire Action Management System

Now it's time to walk you through the exact action management system used to manage my entire life. If you're anything like I am, you have a myriad of business, personal, and family responsibilities that can be overwhelming at times. This system has been a godsend for my life and my productivity.

What I suggest is that you take the next 90 days and follow this exact system for life management. I think you'll be so surprised at how much more productive your life becomes that you'll most likely use it for years to come.

I carry a small physical day planner with me everywhere I go. I know you can use a computer or Personal Digital Assistant (PDA) to manage your tasks, but for me, there's something more real about having all of my responsibilities handwritten on paper. I also take notes just about every day in meetings and on phone calls, so I like having something with me to write in.

I personally carry a planner from Franklin Covey that has two full pages for each day. One page is for notes and the other page has a schedule to put down appointments and a Prioritized Daily Task List (PDTL).

Creating Your Wants List

Every evening before going to bed I write in my PDTL everything I want to get done the next day.

Notice that I said to put down everything I "want" to get done for the next day, not everything I "need" to get done. Here's why I say want instead of need.

In the past I'd look at my long list of things to do and get this negative feeling because everything on the list was a need—not a want. To change my mind-set and look at the list as something positive, I started saying to myself that everything on my list is something I *want* to get done. Remember, never underestimate the power of how your words effect your attitude.

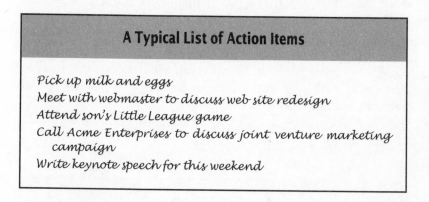

A Typical List of Action Items

Pick up milk and eggs
Meet with webmaster to discuss web site redesign
Attend son's Little League game
Call Acme Enterprises to discuss joint venture marketing campaign
Write keynote speech for this weekend

When you refer to tasks as needs versus wants, your subconscious is going to work out a way for you *not* to be excited about getting them done. When *you* control the programming of your subconscious, you train yourself to be excited about completing the action items.

Easy as ABC

After completing your list, prioritize each activity using three categories: A priorities, B priorities, and C priorities. An A priority represents action items that you absolutely *must* complete; you're not going to go to bed before you have them done. This means being *very* selective about what you list as A priorities.

For the longest time, the overachiever in me would list everything as an A. That meant every day I failed to get all my A priorities done. What happened was that the priorities became meaningless and I had no motivation to get any of the A items done since I never got them all done anyway.

What works best is to limit the A items to the ones that are *absolutely* mandatory for you to get done *today*.

The B priorities are the items that you really *should* get done. They're important, but if you don't complete them today, it's not going to be the end of the world.

Finally, the C priorities are the items that might be important, but it doesn't really matter if you do them today, tomorrow, or next week. Now here's a quick word of caution. If you list *all* your C priorities, this list can get *extremely* long. Put the most important of your C priorities on your daily pages. Then create another list for all the C priority items that you want to get done this month. You can keep this list in the front or back of your planner just to have as a reference. What's worked great for me is putting a blank page at the beginning of each month and listing everything I want to get done for the month.

Prioritizing a List of Action Items

A   Attend son's Little League game
A   Call Acme Enterprises to discuss joint venture marketing campaign
B   Write keynote speech for this weekend
B   Meet with webmaster to discuss web site redesign
C   Pick up milk and eggs

The next step is to number your A, B, and C items in the order you will complete them. I can't stress enough how important this step is. When you have an *order* to complete action items, it gives you a road map to follow and motivates you to take action more than if you just listed them in random order.

Personally, I love starting my day being able to get right down to business and knock them off, one after the other, without having to figure out on the fly which one I should do first, second, third, and so forth.

Let's say you have four A priority items. List them as A1, A2, A3, and A4. When you get to work, you know exactly which one to do first, which one to do second, and so on. After you do that for the As, then you number the Bs—B1, B2, B3, and so on. Then the Cs—C1, C2, C3.

Every day, complete all the A items before you even look at the B items. Complete all the B items before you look at the C items.

As you go through your day, you'll either check the items off, mark them off if you decide not to do them, or carry them over to the next day.

Ordering a Prioritized List of Action Items

A1 Call Acme Enterprises to discuss joint venture marketing campaign
A2 Attend son's Little League game
B1 Meet with webmaster to discuss web site redesign
B2 Write keynote speech for this weekend
C1 Pick up milk and eggs

Timing Is Everything

Here's another step that really took my productivity to another level. Put a time limit next to each A and B priority tasks.

If my first A priority for the day is to plan an agenda for our weekly management conference call, I write "20 min." next to it. If my second A priority might take 30 minutes, I'll write "30 min." next to it.

Once I've done this for all my A and B priority items, I sum up the total time it's going to take to get everything done. That way I can tell if I've listed more things than is possible to get done in a day. When I used to just list everything I *had* to get done that day, I found that it would take more than 24 hours to do them. This exercise keeps you from overestimating what you can accomplish in a day.

Estimating the Time Needed to Complete Each Action Item

45 min.	A1	Call Acme Enterprises to discuss joint venture marketing campaign
2 hrs	A2	Attend son's Little League game
60 min.	B1	Meet with webmaster to discuss web site redesign
1.5 hrs.	B2	Write keynote speech for this weekend
10 min.	C1	Pick up milk and eggs

Scheduling Your Actions

After estimating how long each task will take, write the tasks in your schedule to complete, just like you would for an appointment for a business meeting or a doctor's appointment.

Most people tend to live in reactive mode instead of proactive mode. They let phone calls, e-mails, and coworkers interrupt and distract them until the day is over and they wind up getting nothing done. When you block out specific chunks of time to complete your action items, you'll have total focus, intensity, and control in order to complete what's most important.

If I know I'm going to start work at 10:00 A.M., and I don't have an appointment already scheduled, I'll block out an hour or two exclusively for my A priority items starting at 10:00 A.M. I actually draw a line around this block of time and make sure nothing's going to get in the way of being proactive. With this process, *you* control the day instead of letting the day control you.

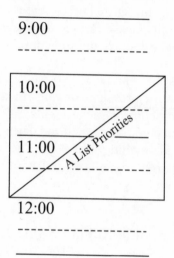

9:00

10:00

11:00

A List Priorities

12:00

E-mail Addiction

Now that you've planned and scheduled your time commitments, the final step is removing as many distractions as possible. One of the biggest time wasters is e-mail.

I strongly encourage you *not* have your e-mail program open all the time. If you're like most people, you might be halfway through a project when you hear your e-mail program "ding" and see that a new message has come through.

It's like an addiction. You just *have* to look at the message. Can you relate? If you break down to read and answer this message, there goes your focus.

Here's what I suggest—*do not* open your e-mail program *at all* until you've completed at least the first few A priority items.

So many of us just can't wait to log on in the morning to see what's waiting in our e-mail box. However, if you simply refuse to even open your e-mail until you've finished a few A priorities, you'll be more motivated to complete the most important items.

Think of retrieving e-mails as a reward for completing items most likely to contribute to your success.

Here's another recommendation. Schedule time to read and respond to e-mails. Limiting this time creates a sense of urgency to get through them all quickly. Personally, I schedule a 45-minute block of time just before lunch and then another hour at the end of the day.

One of the reasons this works so well is because it breaks you of one of the most prevalent diseases in the world—e-mail addiction. If we don't control our time, it's easy to waste it going through e-mails, and before long, half the day is eaten up and you haven't accomplished anything important. Again, take control of your day or your day is going to take control of you.

Set a Time to Plan Your Day

Finally, set aside time to plan your day. I've always found it best to plan at the end of the day right before bed. For me, I have more clarity in the evening when I'm not under pressure to plan out the day in the morning just before getting into action.

While you're planning, paint a mental picture for what you're going to do the next day. As you're sleeping, your mind has time to absorb that mental picture. You'll wake up the next morning with a clear head on the best way to accomplish everything you want to do.

I strongly urge you to try this strategy for the next 90 days. I promise that if followed, you'll be more productive than ever before.

In the next chapter, I'm going to cover one of the most powerful strategies in the world that is going to be a huge multiplier for your success. We're going to talk about the secret characteristic of the world's most powerful people and how you can use it to catapult your level of success.

If you've gotten this far, I'm proud of you! Make sure you've created your dream list and planned how to reach your goals, and I'll see you in the next chapter!

Matt's Action Management Strategy Summary

1. Allocate time every day (such as right before going to bed) where you plan the next day.

2. Make a list of everything you *want* to get done the next day.

3. Prioritize your list into A, B, and C priorities.

4. Arrange A, B, and C priorities in the order you want to complete them.

5. Define a time limit for each A and B priority. Add up the time to make sure you aren't scheduling more than you could possibly complete in a day.

6. Set appointments in your schedule for accomplishing each A and B priority.

7. Schedule time to read and respond to e-mails.

7

The Secret Character Trait of the World's Most Powerful People

If your actions inspire others to dream more, learn more, do more and become more, you are a leader.

—John Quincy Adams

By yourself, you may be the most talented, the most skilled, and the most educated person in the world, but the pinnacle of what you can ultimately accomplish is limited by what you can personally do and achieve every day. That's what makes the saying, "Work smarter, not harder" so important. You only have 24 hours in a day, 7 days in a week, and 12 months out of a year. If you limit your success to your personal efforts, your achievements can only go as high as one person can reach.

The skill that will greatly multiply your success, and the success of those around you, is your leadership.

The amount of success you'll experience is largely determined by your ability to lead and influence others. Everything rises and falls on leadership. Governments, military organizations, corporations, churches, schools, and even your own family will rise to success or plummet to failure based on the skills and abilities of its leader.

When I got started in the entrepreneurial world, I was 18 years old and always looking for this magical "supreme" leader who could mentor me and build me into a success. There's a saying that in order to be a good leader, you must first be a good follower.

The challenge with that statement is that most people stay in the follower role for so long that they develop what I call a "sheep" mentality. A follower who stays in the shadow of his or her leader for too long falls into a comfort zone of mediocrity. By never stepping out of your comfort zone, you never develop your own leadership abilities and also violate the most important principle of leadership.

This principle states that people will generally not follow a leader who has a lower level of leadership than their own. If you're a 7 on the leadership scale of 1 to 10, you typically won't follow someone who's below a 7. Instead, you'll only follow someone who you perceive as higher, such as an 8, 9, or 10 on the leadership scale.

Pay special attention to the careful way I worded that last statement. Did you notice one very important word that makes all the difference in the world as it relates to leadership?

Perceive!

People follow leaders who they "perceive" as a greater leader than themselves. It took me a long time to understand this principle and even longer to put it to use. Luckily, I was blessed with being taught this lesson at a very early stage in my career.

One of the most powerful lessons I've ever received on leadership was from a mentor of mine named Wayne Nugent. Wayne was a leader who struck me with total awe as a public speaker and a leader of thousands of salespeople while being one of the best salespersons I had ever seen. I remember watching him at work and thinking it would take me a lifetime to build myself into the type of leader he was.

To learn as much from him as possible, I religiously applied the principle of "the squeaky wheel gets the grease." That meant I was always calling him and asking him for advice and counseling. I spent hours asking his advice on all aspects of sales and team building. The lessons he shared with me have been a constant guideline over the years no matter what career or industry I chose.

One day after hearing Wayne give a presentation, I told him how much I loved watching him work and how much I wanted to do exactly the same thing. Wayne gave me one of the biggest lessons of my life that has made me grateful to him forever. He said: "Matt, do you want to know the reason why people follow me? There is one reason and one reason only. The reason why I'm a great salesperson, the reason why I'm a great speaker, and the reason why I can recruit the best salespeople to work for me all boils down to one thing that I have more of than anyone I know—*confidence!*"

My response, possibly like your own thoughts right now, was that sounded a little too simple. "But Wayne, you have confidence because you're so good," I replied.

Wayne raised his voice and went on a bit of a tirade. "Dude, don't you get it? I'm so good *because* I have confidence! You can't be a great leader until you're confident you can lead them, you can't motivate someone unless you're confident you'll motivate them, and you can't close someone on a sales call unless you're confident they're going to buy it."

"So how did you get to be so confident?" I asked.

He grinned. "It's simple. I just made the decision one day to project confidence and by projecting confidence, I became a confident person. When I walk into a room, I walk into the room projecting confidence. When I speak to other people, I consciously project confidence in my voice.

"You see, Matt, people are attracted to you as a leader because they see you as stronger and more confident than themselves. People *want* to be led. But they'll only follow leaders who are confident in their ability to lead!

"The only difference between me and everyone else is that I have an insane amount of confidence!"

That hit me like a ton of bricks. From that day forward, I realized that the essence of leadership was simply perception. By projecting myself as more confident than others, I was perceived as having a higher level of leadership.

Of course, it's one thing to believe and feel more confident, but it's an entirely different thing to project that confidence so that others feel it too. I spent a great deal of time watching and modeling confident leaders. I watched what they did and used what I learned to build and project my own confidence.

There are a number of different factors on which people base their initial "gut" feeling as it relates to perceiving someone as a leader. There are entire books dedicated to the topic of body language and perception, but I've narrowed down the most powerful and easiest ways to project confidence through five different factors.

- How you greet someone
- Your voice
- Your posture
- Your facial expressions
- Your wrapping

When meeting someone for the first time, that person is making dozens of instant judgments about you. Some consciously, some unconsciously, but like it or not, we are creatures of judgment. As we all know, first impressions are lasting impressions, so it's important to set a good impression right away.

The customary greeting in most cultures around the world is a handshake. Rule number 1 is to shake hands with a firm grip. If your handshake is weak and soft, you're projecting weakness and softness.

Please, whatever you do, don't get into the toughest grip competition. If you squeeze someone's hand to the degree that it is painful, you don't project confidence, but rather the opposite by overcompensating.

Next, and this is one of the most important factors in how you are immediately perceived as a strong or weak leader, is your eye contact. Many people feel awkward looking someone directly in the eyes upon first meeting them. You can have a firm handshake and the most powerful voice in the world, but if you immediately look away or look down when you greet someone, he or she immediately has a gut sense that you are looking away because of either a lack of self-esteem or that you don't really care, thereby showing a lack of respect.

The point here is not to get into a staring contest, but rather to simply connect with that person, letting he or she know you're comfortable with him or her and you're comfortable with yourself.

The next important factor in your perceived leadership level is your voice. When you meet someone, speak at a slightly louder volume than normal. Case studies have proven that the person with the loudest voice in the group is typically perceived as the leader of that group.

Next, stand with your head up high and with good posture. When you're looking down or slumping your shoulders in public, people perceive you as having a lack of confidence. However, when you stand in a confident manner, your body produces chemicals that actually *do* make you more confident. *Physiology* directly impacts your emotions and your levels of energy.

As a speaker, oftentimes people will pull me aside at a seminar and want to confide in me for some personal counseling. They'll tell me how depressed they are. Interestingly, each and every time they do, you can look at their posture and see them standing with their head down, shoulders slumped, and with a sour look on their face.

My standard response is, "Why have you done that to yourself?" After the normal blank, confused stare, I'll share with them the concept of physiology and how it affects the chemical balance in their body. If they're willing to listen, I'll put them in a different physiological state where it's impossible to feel depressed.

As you read this, I suggest trying this for yourself. Stand tall, put your chest out, hold your head high looking up, put a huge smile on your face, laugh out loud, jump up and down—in that moment, it's impossible to feel depressed because the physiology of your body is producing chemicals that make you feel happy. So start standing with confidence and your mind will start feeling confident.

Next, make a habit of smiling a lot and not showing worry even when things appear difficult. When challenges arise, people look up to their leader to decide how they should react. When they see you smiling and unworried, you project that you're confident in your ability to overcome the challenge. When you have a frown or grimace on your face, you project uncertainty and worry, which causes your people to feel uncertainty and worry.

Finally, make sure you properly "wrap your package." To be perceived as a better leader, dress better than those around you. Whether we want to admit to it or not, perception is reality and when you're dressed nice, not only do you typically feel better about yourself, you gain ground during that crucial first impression.

Once I realized confidence was the key to leadership, that moment became the turning point in my life. That's when I stopped looking for the magical leader and decided to become that leader instead. After learning and applying this lesson, I got started in a direct sales company where my job was to recruit and train a sales team. Previous to this company, I had never achieved any level of success at all. In fact, I felt like I had been a pretty miserable failure. But I decided to follow Wayne's principle and project an extreme level of confidence in everything I did.

When I interviewed salespeople to work for me on a commission-only basis, I started telling them how I would mentor and train them. I started telling them how, when they came on board, I was going to turn them into superstars.

Notice my language. Your words are everything. I used the word *when* they came on board, not *if.* I started using the word *when* because that assumed there was no other option. I eliminated the word "if" because the word "if" projects uncertainty and doubt. I started assuming that every single person I talked to would be crazy to not want to work with me. A strange thing began to happen—people suddenly were telling me how excited they were to work with me!

Before I walked into any meeting, I would say to myself over and over, "Matt, you are the leader that every other leader is looking for." That positive self-talk immediately before a presentation would heighten the level of confidence projected. It was amazing how suddenly I started being followed and perceived as an amazing leader when nothing had changed other than the fact that I began to just take on the role of a leader.

Here's one of the most powerful statements on leadership that you want to always remember—*Power is assumed, not granted!*

Leadership Laws

Over the last 14 years of my entrepreneurial career, having built several million-dollar companies and leading over 100,000 independent salespeople, I've discovered a number of Leadership Laws that have been my guiding principles.

If you don't practice these principles, success becomes very difficult and in many cases impossible. These are not suggestions, recommendations, or generalities; these are specific *laws* that must be followed 100 percent of the time if you want to achieve success as a leader.

- **Leadership Law 1:** The Leader always has a dream larger than those he or she leads.
- **Leadership Law 2:** The Leader always conveys an inspiring vision.
- **Leadership Law 3:** The Leader always has a superior attitude than those he or she leads.
- **Leadership Law 4:** The Leader sets the bar high.
- **Leadership Law 5:** The Leader is a strong decision maker.
- **Leadership Law 6:** The Leader has the highest levels of integrity and character.
- **Leadership Law 7:** The Leader always exhibits persistence and determination.

Leadership Law 1: Have a Dream Larger Than Those You Lead

There is no passion to be found playing small—in settling for a life that is less than the one you are capable of living.

—Nelson Mandela

Big dreamers inspire others to dream big. A leader has to be comfortable communicating his or her dreams through the power of emotional intelligence—the ability to transfer emotion to your organization.

Most aspiring leaders make the mistake of relating leadership qualities to being extremely logical. They may have great management skills, exhibit political correctness, be responsible, and speak eloquently, but none of these factors can override the emotional part of leadership.

People are not moved and influenced by the depth of your logic. They are propelled to action by the height of your passion and inspiration. Most people want to be more than they are and they look for a leader who has a passion for greatness that will inspire them to greatness.

When you get on fire, people will come from miles away to watch you burn!

When you open yourself up and share your dreams, you transfer emotion. People want to be around a leader who's transparent. When they see transparency, not only do you transfer emotion, you also gain their *trust*. You'll never be followed unless you're trusted, and the more open you are, the more trusted you become.

Get a BHAG

Since it doesn't take any more energy to dream big than it does to dream small, create a BHAG . . . a Big, Hairy, Audacious Goal!

When I'm traveling around the world with the speakers and top salespeople in my company, I'm constantly dream building with them. I'm telling them how in just a few years, we'll be flying in our own corporate jet rather than flying commercially.

In talking about your dreams, it's important to paint a picture in their mind of what the experience of that dream will be like. So not only am I talking about flying in our own corporate jet, I'm talking about all the details and telling a story. Facts tell, but stories sell!

Instead of driving a car to the airport, having to be there an hour or two early, going through ticketing, fighting the crowds, going through security to take off our shoes, emptying our pockets, taking off our belts, and then sitting around waiting for our flights, we'll be picked up by a limo. We'll travel over to the private airport where our limo will drive us right up to our jet. We'll never even have to touch our bags—no security, no waiting, no hassles. Our private flight attendant will welcome us with a glass of champagne. If we're tired, we can go to the back of the jet and take a nap. When we land, we'll walk down off the plane into the next limo to whisk us away again.

Now that's painting a picture!

As a leader, you must continually dream build. The more vividly you imagine and picture yourself living these dreams, the more concrete they become in your mind and the more likely you'll turn them into reality.

The reason people buy into a leader's dream is because they see that the leader believes in the dream wholeheartedly. As a leader, you want to crystallize your dreams by visualizing yourself experiencing them over and over to the point where you have absolutely no doubt you'll have them. When you feel that your dreams are within your reach, people around you feel that same energy and want to do anything they can to be part of your dream as well.

Leadership Law 2: Convey an Inspiring Vision

To be blind is bad, but worse is to have eyes and not see.

—Helen Keller

Great leaders are not only comfortable sharing their vision, their passion overflows and spills out to others such that they can't wait to be a part of it. When you share your passion, you transfer that passion to others and inspire them to be greater than they are now. People want to be part of something that makes them feel good about themselves. They want to make a difference in the world and give back. They want to be part of something bigger than themselves. They want to be inspired to move forward with their life and do something remarkable. You must be moving forward because not even a dog will follow a parked car. What do they do to a parked car? I'm sure you guessed it.

Create a vision for your life, for your company, and for your family—share it with passion and enthusiasm.

A vision doesn't just have to be related to business. Personally, I have a vision for my family because I believe families rise and fall based on leadership. That's why I'm constantly sharing my vision with my wife, Rhonda, and our newborn daughter, Zara. I tell Zara how we're going to take her all over the world so she can learn history not just in books, but by actually going to the places in the world that most kids only read about.

I'm constantly telling her how much we love her, how we're going to support her in all her dreams and goals, how smart she is, how proud of her we are, and how we have the most amazing and loving family in the world. I believe with everything in me that even babies are influenced by your vision.

With Rhonda, I'm always telling her how we're going to make a massive contribution to the world, how we're going to raise wonderful children, how she's the best mom in the world, how we're going to live out all our dreams and goals, and how much I love and adore her for supporting our vision.

Far too many families live by the philosophy that their success both financially, spiritually, and even in their love and harmony, is going to happen by chance. It doesn't work that way. Your family's success is going to come from *leading* your family to success. I don't want to sound sexist or anything, but men, I believe your partner wants to see your strength and your leadership. Rhonda and I have been together for over six years now and I believe that one of the reasons we have such a great relationship that keeps getting stronger is because Rhonda knows I'm going to do everything in my power to lead our family to success in every area I possibly can.

Use a Different Carrot

In business, far too many leaders use mere dollars as the carrot to motivate their people to action. What happens when you use money as the biggest motivator is that people will leave you in a second if they can earn more money somewhere else. Money, you see, is a fairly shallow motivator. If money is your carrot, you have no competitive advantage because that's the primary motivator that everyone else uses.

One of my rules of success is to always be a contrarian. If everyone else is using money as his or her primary motivator, do something else! By looking in new directions, you can often find a new path to success that others overlook. John D. Rockefeller even said, "If you want to succeed, you should strike out on new paths rather than travel the worn paths of accepted success."

If you look at many of the truly great companies in the world, you'll see that their leaders inspired them to go after an inspiring vision.

Take the example of Microsoft founder Bill Gates. Back in the mid-1980s, Bill Gates set a goal to have Microsoft software running on a personal computer on the desk of every person in the world. At the time, that was an unheard of goal since most personal computers were not only expensive, but too complicated for most people to use.

To reach this ambitious goal, Bill Gates had Microsoft develop a program, called Windows, to make personal computers much simpler and friendlier to use. Then Microsoft adopted their most popular productivity programs to run on Windows, such as their word processor (Word), spreadsheet (Excel), presentation program (PowerPoint), and database (Access). The combination of popular productivity programs, combined with Windows making computers easier to use, gave more people a reason to buy a personal computer and use Microsoft's software.

Today, over 90 percent of all computers run some form of Microsoft software. Microsoft dominates the software industry because Bill Gates had the vision to see where he wanted to take his company and the courage to do what it took to get there.

Life is short; we all have a very limited time on this planet. My belief is that if you want to experience fulfillment, it will not be created through any amount of money you earn but by the impact you make in this world.

Leadership Law 3: Always Have a Superior Attitude

Courage is going from failure to failure without losing enthusiasm.

—Winston Churchill

I once heard that "50 percent of your success is attitude. The other 50 percent is attitude!"

There are, of course, many other factors that contribute to success, but the one characteristic of truly great leaders is that they have an unyielding positive attitude toward the success of their organization.

Attitude control is a constant battle. As a leader, you want to feed yourself as much as you possibly can with powerful thoughts and be upbeat in front of the people you lead.

Every leader is going to experience disappointment, discouragement, and challenges that may seem insurmountable. While those may be feelings in your heart, great leaders must keep those negative feelings to themselves. And yes, it's a tough job some days.

When people see you visibly discouraged, they feel a greater sense of discouragement. When they see you visibly worried, they feel a greater sense of worry. Negative emotions from a leader produce nothing but negative results in their people.

Remember, leaders have an amazing ability to transfer emotion to their people, both negatively and positively. Negative emotions from you as the leader transfer those negative emotions to your people. Negative emotions in your people create negative results in productivity and loyalty.

Positive emotions from you as the leader transfer positive emotions to your people. Positive emotions in your people create positive results in productivity and loyalty.

People want to be surrounded by people who make them feel good. Great leaders have an amazing ability to make people feel better about themselves. A major way to do that is through your positive energy.

A true leader sees the solution and doesn't focus on the problems. Your people look to you to help them overcome challenges as they arise. When you're upbeat and positive, despite the obstacles in front of you, you emote confidence and inspire people to move forward. Positive attitudes are just as contagious as negative ones. But always remember, negative attitudes spread 10 times faster than positive ones!

Leadership Law 4: Set the Bar High

The quality of a person's life is in direct proportion to their commitment to excellence, regardless of their chosen field of endeavor.

—Vince Lombardi

Another cardinal rule in leadership is that "the speed of the group is determined by the speed of the leader."

A manager tells others how to do it and sits back and watches. A leader shows people how to do it and sets the example.

Poor work habits by the leader will produce the same poor work habits in the organization. It's like the old saying, "What parents do in moderation, children tend to do in excess." To set the right example for your organization you must take the lead!

In most cases, the group of people you lead will look to you (as their leader) to determine psychologically what level of productivity they will achieve. You set the bar as to the highest level they will aspire. It's not that they can't work harder than you, produce more sales than you, or any other task that would be customary in your line of leadership. In fact, as you grow as a truly great leader, you'll start to attract leaders who *will* outperform you, but until then, set the bar and set it high.

One example of this rule occurred when I was 24 years old and became a sales director in a travel company. In my first month with the company, I went out and personally sold 30 travel club memberships in 30 days, in addition to building my sales team. It was the company record and not one single person in my sales team surpassed me.

I went into sales management mode and was working with my salespeople more than I was making personal sales. After about four or five months of this, I started to get frustrated. Month after month had gone by, but not one person in my entire sales team had made more than 30 sales. I had several who had done more than 20, but none had done 30 or more. I had set the bar at 30.

I decided to do a little experiment. Rather than continue to "manage" my team, I decided I would be a leader and set the example to raise the bar to a new level.

The next month, I went on a selling frenzy. I did whatever it took to push my sales up to over 40 personal sales by the end of the month.

Amazingly, an interesting thing happened. I was managing my team less than I was previously, but all of a sudden everyone's production went up. Rather than have several people who sold memberships in the twenties, just under my previous level of 30, I had several people who had surpassed my original record of 30 and some even got close to 40!

Nothing changed other than the fact that, psychologically, my sales team saw that it was possible to make more than 30 sales. You see, people have a paradigm set in their mind. The role of a leader is to break that paradigm, which, in turn, inspires confidence in others to believe they can do more than they originally thought possible.

Perhaps the most dominant example of a leader breaking through people's mental limitations is the example of Roger Bannister breaking the four-minute mile.

For years, it was assumed that it was physically impossible for a man to run a mile in less than four minutes. Hundreds of people tried breaking this mythical four-minute mile, but time after time, they could never break through this time limit until everyone assumed that this time limit was a well-known and accepted fact.

That's when Roger Bannister shocked the world by running a mile under four minutes. Within weeks, several other people quickly broke the four-minute mile limit as well. The secret wasn't that the four-minute mile was a physical barrier, but rather a mental one. The moment other people saw Roger Bannister succeed, they believed they could succeed, too, and they did.

Roger Bannister might not have known it, but he was being a true leader. By breaking the four-minute mile barrier himself, he proved by example what was truly possible so that others could follow in his path. True leaders lead by example and make it easy for others to see what's possible. When others are inspired by your actions, that's when you'll know you've reached a new level in your own leadership ability.

Leadership Law 5: Be a Strong Decision Maker

In a moment of decision the best thing you can do is the right thing. The worst thing you can do is nothing.

—Theodore Roosevelt

Nothing is more frustrating than a leader who cannot make a decision to act. Too many managers focus on analyzing every decision to the nth degree and continually miss opportunities because they were simply too slow to act.

Someone once said that a manager is concerned with doing things right, but a leader is concerned with doing the right thing.

Not all of your decisions will be correct. In fact, many times you'll make wrong decisions more often than you would like. But as long as you're making them and making them for the right reasons, you'll learn to make right decisions more often. Your decisions will get better as you gain experience.

Remember to strive for excellence, not perfection. A quote that has stuck with me for years was from the founder of IBM, Thomas Watson. Mr. Watson was once asked what the secret to success was. Watson replied, "It's quite simple, really. Double your rate of failure. You're thinking of failure as the enemy of success. But it isn't at all."

Leaders often make the wrong decisions. But a true leader is man or woman enough to go ahead and make the tough decisions anyway.

Perhaps the most famous example of someone who failed often on their way to success is Thomas Edison. When Thomas Edison was only seven years old, he attended school for three months before his teacher labeled him a slow learner. His mother pulled him out of school and taught him at home, where he quickly developed an interest in science.

While working as a telegraph operator for Western Union near Wall Street, Edison repaired the Gold Exchange's new telegraphic gold-price indicator after it broke down. After studying how the crude stock ticker worked, he set about inventing a better one, which earned him $40,000 for his invention, known as the Edison Universal Stock Printer.

At the age of 20, Edison set up his famous laboratory in Menlo Park, New Jersey, as a full-time inventor. In one year alone, he earned over 400 patents for his various inventions, which caused the local citizens to nickname him "The Wizard of Menlo Park."

Perhaps Edison's greatest triumph occurred in 1878 when he announced to the world that he would invent an inexpensive electric light to replace the gas light. Ridiculed over his prediction, Edison experimented with over 10,000 different materials until he finally invented the first incandescent lightbulb on October 21, 1879.

Thomas Edison knew that the road to success is paved with failure. Without failure, you can never succeed. In reflecting back on his experiment to develop the lightbulb, Edison even stated, "I have not failed. I've just found 10,000 ways that won't work."

As a leader, be assured that failure is only a disaster if you quit. If you learn from your mistakes, failure just becomes another stepping stone to your ultimate goal.

Leadership Law 6: Commit to Integrity and Character

Only a man's character is the real criterion of worth.

—Eleanor Roosevelt

First, let's define integrity. Integrity is the quality of being honest and having strong moral principles. Nothing breaks an organization down faster than when the leader is willing to sacrifice morality for money. If a leader is willing to lie, cheat, or steal to get ahead, success is always short-term because no one will continue following someone who does not lead with integrity. Leaders who refuse to sacrifice their principles end up being followed for decades.

If a company grows with integrity, and lives by the philosophy of *People before Profits*, it builds a foundation for long-term stability by instilling a sense of loyalty among its customers and employees.

Another definition of integrity is the condition of being whole and undivided. It's being the same person when you're in front of your organization as you are when the organization isn't around. People can always sense someone who's putting on a façade just so he or she can look good.

Here's a cardinal rule: Never talk behind anyone's back in your organization. When someone hears you bad-mouthing a colleague when he or she is not around, that person will wonder if you also bad-mouth him or her. When people in your organization have even the slightest hint that's a possibility, they will *not* follow you.

When you always do the right thing, your team sees that. They have confidence and faith and will follow you through thick and thin, no matter what the circumstances are. No other leadership principle is as important as integrity.

I've been fortunate enough to have a group of leaders who I've worked with for almost ten years now, and the reason we've stuck together for almost a decade is because we trust each other. We know that we have each other's back, and we know that if we say we're going to do something, we will always honor our word to the greatest of our abilities.

Leadership Law 7: Persistence and Determination

Press on. Nothing can take the place of persistence. Talent will not; the world is full of unsuccessful people with talent. Genius will not; unrewarded genius is almost a proverb. Education alone will not; the world is full of educated derelicts. Persistence and determination alone are omnipotent.

—Calvin Coolidge

Greatness takes time to achieve. In my first two to three years as an entrepreneur, I wound up $30,000 in debt and homeless. But because I persisted despite my failures, I made it over the hump to create an amazing life.

Because I didn't give up, I haven't had to think about money in years, because it's just not a concern. If I want to take my wife to Paris for the weekend, spend $1,000 a night on a suite in a hotel because it's her birthday, buy her a $3,000 necklace (which I did on Valentine's Day), or write an $11,000 check to charity (which we did a few months ago), I don't even have to think twice about it because it's such a low percentage of our income.

I shudder to think of where my life would be if I had given up after failing initially. I would never have been able to experience this kind of lifestyle.

Here's what's important about a true leader: A true leader will always find a way over, around, or through any challenge that arises and will do whatever it takes to be a winner.

Successful people do what unsuccessful people are unwilling to do. Winners in life just don't give up. Winners don't throw in the towel when times get tough. Winners will never, *ever* let *anyone* steal their dream!

The Secret Character Trait of the World's Most Successful People

People are always blaming their circumstances for what they are. I don't believe in circumstances. The people who get on in this world are the people who get up and look for circumstances they want, and, if they can't find them, MAKE THEM.

—George Bernard Shaw

Without exception, I can talk to a complete stranger and in less than five minutes, determine that person's level of success just by asking one simple question:

"What is your biggest failure in life?"

If she, for example, complains and tells me about someone else dropping the ball, or how her partner did her wrong, or how it was someone else's fault, I instantly know she is nowhere close to being where she wants in life because she's holding herself powerless. When you blame others, you take your own power completely away.

Here's what I finally realized. Every time I tried shifting responsibility to someone or something else, I was being a spineless little wimp.

You see, we all have the same amount of power; it's just deciding if you want to use your power negatively or positively. When you shift blame, the only thing you're saying is, "Let me be powerless."

From this day forward, realize that when you make excuses, you're basing your results, your success, your freedom, and your livelihood on something else. When something else other than you is in control, you are weak. You have no power. But when you take 100 percent responsibility, you are strong, you have power, and you gain the ability to control your destiny.

By accepting 100 percent responsibility for their actions, leaders gain the confidence to persist in moving toward their goals. They may not move as fast as they like and they may encounter more obstacles than they expected, but they simply persist until they literally force their way to a solution and reach their ultimate goal.

The mark of a true leader and the secret character trait of the world's most powerful people is taking 100 percent responsibility.

Part II

Becoming an Unemployed Millionaire

8

Starting a Business

Success is not the key to happiness. Happiness is the key to success. If you love what you are doing, you will be successful.

—Albert Schweitzer

Many of you reading this book may already have a business, or at least have a business idea. However, if you're like I was when I first got started, I had no idea what business I wanted to start, just that I wanted to be in business for myself.

Just because you may not have experience selling a particular product or service doesn't mean you can't succeed in that type of business. When I started my first Internet marketing business, for example, I had never had an online business and had never marketed *anything* online before. I had *zero* experience.

But it was something that interested and excited me. More importantly, it was something I believed I could succeed with. If there's one element that's more important than any others, it's the word "belief." Whether you believe you can, or you believe you can't, you're right.

Before going through the process of helping you decide what kind of business to start, I'd like to cover a few things that are even more important because they are the foundational character traits of almost every incredibly successful businessperson I've worked with or interviewed over the years.

False Illusions

One of the biggest pitfalls I see with new entrepreneurs is that they have this dream in their mind of how their business is going to be. They think about how wonderful it will be to be their own boss. They make wild projections as to how much money will roll in without accounting for the many challenges that are sure to come. Sadly, because they experience these challenges early on, they give up long before they achieve any level of success.

More important than any business idea or strategic plan are your core character traits, as they relate to your success in business. Those elements are your *burning desire* and *dogged determination* to be successful—no matter what it takes.

Besides desire and the determination to win in business, as I mentioned earlier in the book, you'll also need to have a big dream and be ready to get knocked around. When I was new to business, I believed starting a business was far less challenging than it really was and didn't consider the many downturns I would face. These pesky challenges kept coming up and I thought, "poor me." I had the mind-set that I had bad luck because so many problems kept getting in my way.

My saving grace was the pig-headed determination to get through these obstacles. One of the major reasons, if not the main reason, why 90 percent of all businesses fail is because business owners do not properly anticipate the inevitable barrage of challenges ahead. Although you can never identify all of the challenges that your business may face, you need to know that they *will* come. You can hope and wish all day long that you won't have to go through them, but I can guarantee they'll always arise. Starting any business means facing and solving problems every day.

The best advice on problems I can give was shared with me by a businessman one day:

Rather than hope you won't face any problems, expect and appreciate them.

When you expect and appreciate problems, you're able to stay out of the "poor me" syndrome that produces nothing but negative results.

Let's break these two down:

1. *Expect problems:* By expecting problems, you develop a mind-set that they're completely normal and just a routine aspect of being in business. When the problems are seen as routine, you won't burn yourself out with stress and you'll be able to develop a positive mind-set to tackle negatives whenever they appear.

2. *Be grateful for problems:* The gratitude was a bit harder for me to embrace. Being *grateful* for problems seemed absurd. But after digging a bit deeper, I was able to realize two important reasons to have gratitude. First, I'm grateful that God has given me challenges to have in the first place. The majority of the population is stuck in a miserable existence, slaves to someone else for most of their lives. If I have to go through a few challenges to have the freedom to live life on my terms, I'm truly grateful for that.

    The second reason I'm grateful comes from what Mom always told me growing up: "What doesn't kill you makes you stronger." Or as they said in the Marine Corps, "Pain is just weakness leaving the body." Every challenge that comes along makes you a better businessperson. The greater your challenges, the greater level of knowledge and leadership you'll attain.

If you desire to be your own boss, live life on your terms, and become an Unemployed Millionaire, embrace your challenges and thank God for them. Do this and I can promise that not only will your life be a lot easier and more fulfilled, but you'll have the mind-set of persistence to build a great future.

Again, remember the most important character trait for realizing your dreams is your *burning desire* and *dogged determination* to win.

Early in my business career, I went through so many challenges that I wanted to give up. What kept me going was the desire to become a millionaire and live the lifestyle of my dreams. When the going got tough, I wrote out four letters on a postcard. Anytime I got discouraged, I looked at that postcard with those four simple letters—"W.E.I.T."—to remind me that I had to do "*What Ever It Takes*" to be a success.

Follow Your Passion

If you're going to go into business for yourself, get into a business that you're passionate about. In most cases, especially in the beginning, you'll spend more hours on your business than you may like. If you're passionate about your business, these extra hours won't feel like extra work. Instead, those extra hours will feel more like an adventure.

For years, I was involved in businesses that I wasn't incredibly passionate about, but they were a great source of income. Even though I wasn't really passionate about past businesses that generated millions of dollars (online selling web sites and leads), I used those businesses to make money. But the real benefit was that it showed me what I did enjoy, which was the creative side of marketing. Once you know what you like and dislike about a particular business, you can narrow your business choices to focus on your greatest passion while minimizing anything you don't like.

In many cases, your first business won't be the perfect business for you. What your first business can show you is what parts of business you do enjoy. In many cases you won't know exactly what you like or dislike until you actually begin to run your business. That's why it's important not to hesitate or wait to start and run a business. Every business will be a learning experience for you so the key is to get started.

Oddly enough, you'll be surprised at how fast your happiness and income can rise once you truly identify a business you're completely passionate about. When I finally made the decision to pursue my true passion, my success skyrocketed to an entirely new level.

I still remember the experience of sitting down one day to figure out what I wanted to do with the rest of my life. Honestly, I had gotten a bit bored with what I was doing and wanted to find something I knew could be exciting for the next 20-plus years of my life.

I had spent several years chasing the money instead of chasing my passion. So I made the decision that I would simply refuse to get into any business, no matter what the potential income was, if I wasn't passionate about it.

That simple experience of committing to pursue my passions above all else allowed me to go from generating a little over a million a year to almost $10 million a year in revenue in a very short time. My success was multiplied by a factor of about 10 simply because I loved what I did.

Before you start any business, ask yourself a few questions first:

What am I most passionate about?

What do I know about?

What do people ask me advice about?

What am I really good at doing?

What do I have experience doing?

What do I think about all the time?

What do I love talking about?

Whether it's experience from a job, skills you developed from a hobby, or simply something that you talk about because it interests you, each are important elements that can help determine what kind of business to pursue.

Remember, there is no single "best" way to become an Unemployed Millionaire. Everyone has different interests, strengths, and desires. Ultimately, you have to find your own path to success.

Everyone has a different passion, which forms the underlying foundation to become an Unemployed Millionaire. When you infuse your life with what you're most passionate about, life suddenly becomes so exciting that money is actually irrelevant.

Now don't get me wrong. I want you to become a millionaire and you'll never hear me say money is not important. What I mean by money being irrelevant is that when you do what you love, you can focus on building that love (instead of the money) but still earn a fortune.

It's unfortunate, but many entrepreneurs earn millions of dollars and find themselves so completely unhappy, they literally throw it all away. When you're truly happy doing what you want and working toward a passionate desire, you'll have a solid foundation for making more money than you ever believed possible. Passion is what drives true success in every endeavor.

Passion infuses your life with so many positive qualities:

- It gives your life meaning and purpose.
- It gives your life direction.
- It gives you strength to overcome problems and obstacles.
- It makes your life fun and exciting.

As soon as you find your passion, you'll find that life takes on a whole different feel. Just think of going to bed as a kid, knowing that tomorrow would be your birthday party. Just thinking about this probably made you excited about the next day.

Since passion is so important, you can't afford one more day without clearly identifying your greatest desire. Once you find that dream that can motivate you every day without fail, your life will never be the same again.

Here are some ways to identify what you might be most passionate about:

- If you had all the money in the world and could do anything you wanted, what would you do?
- If you knew that you couldn't fail, what would you do?

- What do you enjoy doing most with your free time?
- What are you good at that other people ask for your advice?
- What is the common topic of your favorite books, magazines, and TV shows?
- What do you enjoy most about your current job?

Before you read any further, answer the previous questions—your future literally depends on what you write down.

I've always been passionate about personal development because it helped me climb out of debt when I was homeless and living out of my car. I made the decision that I would start a company in the personal development industry to get the same information that changed my life into the hands of others around the world.

Once I determined what I was passionate about, I then had to decide exactly how I would bring my company to market to turn that passion into profits. I could have applied this passion in many different directions. I could have pursued a career solely as a motivational speaker, started a speaker's bureau to promote motivational speakers, become a personal development coach, run a coaching company, started a company that would train corporations, or any number of other businesses in the personal development industry. I chose to channel my passion into starting Success University, which delivers personal development training from over 100 of the top speakers and trainers all over the world through the power of the Internet. I found a way to both follow my passion and turn that passion into millions of dollars.

Another passion of mine has been to make a difference in feeding hungry children around the world who, without our support, would otherwise face an almost certain death. Currently there are over 30,000 children who die every day because of hunger and treatable diseases. It's a crisis that I know we have the resources to eradicate in our lifetime. I also believe that if you're not part of the solution, you're part of the problem.

In my effort to be part of the solution, I implemented a fundraising program with my company where a small percentage of our sales go to Feed The Children. If you don't know who Feed The Children is, it is an organization that's been responsible for saving the lives of millions of children around the world.

Larry and Frances Jones started Feed The Children in 1979 and since then have reached out to help children and families in 118 countries around the globe. In 2008 they shipped 135 million pounds of food and other essentials around the world and supplemented almost 800,000 meals a day worldwide.

Although I've only made a small contribution in the grand scheme of things, by simply having a small percentage of our revenues go to Feed The Children, my company has been responsible for donating enough money to feed tens of thousands of children.

How do you want to fulfill your passion? There is no simple answer because the answer is different for everybody. The key is to create a business you could realistically see yourself being happy with for the next 20 years. However you want to channel your passion depends on what you want to do with your life.

Work Is Love Made Visible

No one can succeed in any endeavor that they don't like.
If you don't love what you're doing, then don't do it.

Your chances of success are directly proportional
to the degree of pleasure you derive from what you do.

Do something that you have a deep personal interest in.
Do something you'd enjoy spending twelve to fifteen hours a day
working at, and the rest of the time thinking about.

Don't set compensation as your goal.
Find work you like and the compensation will follow.

Work is not your punishment.
It's your reward, your strength and your pleasure.

Real success is achieved when you like what you do.
When your vocation becomes your vacation,
you never work another day in your life.

—Author Unknown

Getting Started

You may agree that passion is important in anyone's life, and you may understand that channeling your passion into action can bring you happiness, but you may wonder why so few people seem to pursue their dreams. More importantly, you may wonder how you can pursue your own dreams.

To pursue your dreams, the first step is to commit to change. We all get into habits that are easy to follow but require conscious effort to break, like eating the wrong foods, biting your nails, or smoking. Our habits are like slipping on a pair of comfortable shoes. The key is to commit to doing the things necessary to move you toward success so that these become new habits in your life.

If you want to change anything in your life, you must stop or do less of something that you already do to make room for something new. For example, if you want to get into shape, you not only have to create a new exercise habit, but you also have to eliminate or cut back on something that presently fills your time.

Maybe you'll need to wake up an hour earlier every day. Perhaps you might spend less time watching TV at night, or eliminate this habit altogether. You might need to take a shorter lunch and use that time to exercise at a gym. Whenever we add something new to our life, something else has to go.

If you're stuck in a job you don't like and decide to become an Unemployed Millionaire, guess what? Initially, you'll have to make some sacrifices and change a few of your habits. You'll probably have to continue working in your job while following an Unemployed Millionaire business model. If you decide to go into network marketing, you may need to take time during the evenings and weekends to attend meetings or conference calls. If you decide to pursue real estate investing, looking at different properties will take time. If you go into Internet marketing, you may need to spend time learning the latest marketing techniques and applying them to your web site.

There's always an initial cost in time no matter what you choose to do. That's why you'll want to choose something you're passionate about. If you're passionate about getting into shape, your passion will keep your eyes focused on the goal of feeling great and being healthy. If you hate getting into shape, you'll just stay curled up in a warm bed and sleep in another half hour. If you're passionate about improving your life, then cutting back on your habits won't seem like a hardship, but a step forward to experience life more fully. You see, without passion, starting something new when your schedule is crowded can be daunting.

That's the number one reason why so many people fail to keep their New Year's resolutions. It's not that they don't want to achieve their goals, but that those goals don't generate enough passion in their lives. To most people, New Year's resolutions are something that would be nice to have, but aren't worth fighting for. Choosing a goal that excites you allows you to enjoy the journey along the way to success.

You Either Take Risks or You're at Risk

In the old days, life was much simpler. You went to school, got a good job, retired, and collected a pension so you could enjoy your golden years. Nowadays, this plan no longer works.

As I write this, the national unemployment figure is creeping up to 10 percent, the stock market is nosediving and sinking everyone's retirement accounts, home foreclosures are at their highest peak in decades, and even major companies like General Motors and CitiGroup are teetering on the edge of bankruptcy. If you thought you could rely on a job, your pension or 401K, or even your house to provide you with security, you're in for a rude awakening.

Don't think that a formal education will help either. By no means am I anti-education. If I had to do it all over again, I would probably have finished college. I will be doing everything in my power to ensure my children graduate from college. I believe college teaches a great amount of discipline and gives the majority of graduates a great foundation for their future learning. But the prospect of a degree ensuring your security is a complete falsehood.

The U.S. Department of Labor estimates that the average American will change careers (not just jobs) 10 times during his or her lifetime. If the average graduate enters the workforce at age 22 and retires at age 65, that leaves only 43 years to work.

That means if you spend time and money earning a typical four-year college degree, in 4.3 years you'll probably change careers. Now all your past education may have little to do with your new career, which means another endless cycle of more education that will last just a few short years before that becomes obsolete as well.

Control Your Own Destiny

The answer is simple. You absolutely must control your own destiny. You can't rely on the government to bail you out since even Social Security may go bankrupt. You can't rely on any company to provide security for you since even major corporations are cutting back, downsizing, and going out of business. The only person you can rely on is yourself.

If you want the lifestyle that you've always fantasized about, the only reliable path to that dream is to go into business for yourself.

Why Invent the Average When You Can Copy Genius?

Fools learn from experience. I prefer to learn from the experience of others.

—Otto von Bismarck

While it's important to follow your passion and market a product or service that you're excited about, make sure you have a hungry market to sell to. One of the biggest mistakes new entrepreneurs make is the belief that they need to come up with something that's "breakthrough" or "revolutionary." They'll look online and see that somebody else is doing something similar, or nearly identical, to their idea and get discouraged and give up.

Here's the reality: *If nobody else is doing what you want to do, there's probably a reason!* Rather than see competition as a barrier to your success, look at competition as proof that your idea is worth pursuing in the first place.

You don't need a breakthrough or revolutionary product that will change the world. All you need is a good product backed by superior marketing and service. You also don't need to be a pioneer. There are countless cases of entrepreneurs who have simply studied what works, improved upon it, and made a fortune.

Consider the humble beginnings of Bill Gates and Microsoft. Whatever you may think of Bill Gates, you cannot deny that he succeeded in becoming the richest man on the planet. Initially, he went to Harvard to study law, but after a few years of college, he found a bigger passion in the fledgling personal computer market.

Turning his back on a secure and lucrative career as a lawyer, Gates instead decided to start his own computer company writing software for personal computers. His first product was a program that made it easy for anyone to program a personal computer.

About this time, IBM was planning to develop its own personal computer and needed software to make it work. After contacting a much larger software company, IBM next contacted Microsoft. Sensing an opportunity, Gates told IBM that he could deliver the necessary software within the timeline that IBM needed.

IBM agreed and signed a contract. Unknown to IBM, Mr. Gates had no such software, nor was his young company capable of producing such software in the limited time available.

At this point, Bill Gates started looking for other companies that had the software he needed. He soon found a programmer selling a program dubbed QDOS, which stood for Quick and Dirty Operating System. Bill Gates purchased the rights to QDOS for only $50,000 and renamed it Microsoft Disk Operating System or MS-DOS. This one program would eventually earn Microsoft millions of dollars and became the predecessor to Microsoft Windows, the most dominant operating system in the personal computer market.

Bill Gates didn't try to create his own operating system. He simply found one that worked, bought it, improved it, and made it into his own. The real genius of Bill Gates wasn't that he was necessarily a brilliant programmer, but that he was a brilliant businessman. He knew that given a choice between trying to create something from scratch or buying something that already existed, it was much faster and more cost-effective to improve upon something that already worked.

Modeling

The previous example shows why I'm a big believer in a concept called modeling. Modeling is a simple formula that says to be hugely successful, find people who have experienced the results you want. Then figure out how they did it, do the exact same thing, and get similar if not identical results.

When I started my first online business, I was selling travel club memberships and training independent salespeople to do the same through a direct sales company. We sold through personal contacts, referrals, running ads in newspapers, and handing out flyers. Typically we would do our sales presentations in offices, hotel meetings, or private lunch meetings at restaurants.

Because I was always looking to further expand our reach, I started looking online for additional ways to market. I found another direct sales company that used a different way to generate sales. Rather than simply directing people to a web site that explained the benefits of owning the product, they required people to fill in their name, phone number, and e-mail address as a way to get additional information. Then, and only then, could the prospect read additional information on the product.

Initially this seemed a bit strange because you would naturally think that a lot fewer people would fill out their personal information just to read about a product. I discovered that was 100 percent true, but the ones who did were much more qualified and truly interested. Because they had given their phone number, one of our salespeople could follow up to present more information over the phone.

In addition, they could be sent e-mails following up with them every few days with more reasons to buy the product. When I first got involved in sales, I learned that you had to follow up with the average person five to seven times before he or she decided to buy. So while a lot less people filled out their personal information, the closing rate was exponentially higher than just sending people to a web site. (Note: I'll be teaching more about this strategy in Chapter 11, "Internet Marketing," to show you how you can do the same thing with your marketing.)

Today, this is a strategy used by tens of thousands of companies marketing online, but at the time this was a fairly new concept. Because I had learned the concept of modeling, I thought it would probably work with my product as well. Not only could I use this to sell travel club memberships, I could offer it to my salespeople as a tool.

Since I didn't have a ton of money to invest in starting an online company, I had to find partners who were willing to invest their time and knowledge in exchange for future profits. I tapped into my resource of friends and contacts to find someone who could work with me starting this business since my online knowledge consisted of sending e-mails.

One friend of mine had a wealth of knowledge setting up and designing web sites. He also had a friend who was a programmer. The three of us, with no more than a few thousand dollars in capital, were off and running to start our business.

I designed the overall marketing flow of the web site and the sales process while my partners designed the web site, got it hosted online, and handled all the programming. Within about 60 days we were ready for business. Then an amazing thing happened—it worked!

Within about six months, we were generating over $100,000 a month online. If I had to boil that success down to one strategy, it was not just the modeling concept alone. It came from what I call Modeling and Improving. I simply modeled an idea from somewhere else, tweaked and improved it for my particular product, and created a new marketing tool without having to reinvent the wheel in the process.

Look at your own business idea. What can you model from your competitors? What can you model from fields completely unrelated to your business? If you keep your eyes open, you're sure to find a suitable model that you can improve and apply to your own business. You'll save time and money and possibly make a fortune to boot.

Dealing with Competition

As long as you've chosen a product that is in demand in the marketplace, you can be assured that other companies will appear to compete against you. Many entrepreneurs get worried about competitors, but here's a secret that you should adopt immediately to make you love having competition. You can look at competitors one of two ways, from a scarcity mentality or an abundance mentality.

The scarcity mentality envisions competitors taking business away from you. In a traditional business, that is 100 percent true. Look at Wal-Mart as the perfect example of why *not* to get involved in a traditional brick and mortar business. Everywhere Wal-Mart goes, it drives local businesses out of the market.

The second way to look at competition is from an abundance mindset. Competition should be embraced and looked at as a positive for two main reasons. First, the simple fact that you have competitors says that you're in an industry large enough to warrant them. My philosophy is that competitors help create more awareness for my products and make my job even easier because all I need to do is implement a few strategies to put myself ahead of them.

The other reason competition is so valuable? You can learn every trick of your competitors. When I see something effective from a competitor, I look for ways to take that strategy, make it even better, and apply it to my own business.

Who, What, and How

Whether you're in business already, or if you just want to start a business, start with a competitive analysis so you'll know where you stand. The three main parts of competitive intelligence involves understanding *who* is the competition, *what* they do, and *how* they do it.

Knowing your competition is an idea as old as 500 B.C., when the great Chinese military strategist, Sun Tzu, wrote *The Art of*

War. His philosophies are still relevant for today's business leaders. Study these famous quotes from Sun Tzu as a guiding philosophy to win against your competitors:

- "Know the enemy and know yourself; in a hundred battles you will never be in peril."
- "When you are ignorant of the enemy and know yourself, your chances of winning or losing are equal."
- "If ignorant both of your enemy and of yourself, you are certain in every battle to be in peril." (p. 84)

Who

The "who" part of competitive intelligence simply means studying one or more businesses that compete, directly or indirectly, with your own. It's often easy to find businesses that are direct competitors. For example, if you run a movie theater, your direct competitors are other movie theaters. What can be trickier is identifying indirect competitors.

An indirect competitor to a movie theater is a video rental store. Others might include Netflix or Redbox, which now allows you to pick up DVD rentals from over 12,000 vending machines. Still another indirect competitor could be concerts, plays, comedy clubs, and other forms of entertainment that cause customers to spend money elsewhere. Every business has a handful of direct competitors, but they also have dozens more indirect competitors. These are the competitors you need to watch especially closely because if they blindside you, they can steal your business away before you know it.

Indirect competitors can not only steal your customers, but they can wipe out your industry altogether. At one time, railroad companies viewed only other railroad companies as competitors for passengers. Then the airlines appeared and killed the passenger train industry. You risk the same fate if you don't study your indirect competitors.

Doing a competitive analysis identifies the strengths and weaknesses of competitors within your market. Knowing this, you will discover key strategies for a distinct advantage over all competition, both direct and indirect.

What

The "what" part of competitive intelligence involves understanding what your competitors do. For example, identify what services or products your competitors offer and ask yourself if you can offer those services or products, too. What type of advertising and marketing do your competitors use? What is your competition's greatest advantage?

The more you know about your competition, the more you can mimic what your competition does and either improve upon it or look for weaknesses in your competition's business model. For example, if your competitor regularly e-mails a newsletter to prospects and customers, figure out a way to make your newsletter better or more entertaining, such as branding it as a "video" newsletter. With today's technology, it's incredibly affordable to film a series of quick videos and include a link to your video that can be hosted through any number of free video hosting web sites.

Some popular and free video hosting sites include:

- YouTube (www.youtube.com)
- Viddler (www.viddler.com)
- Google Video (www.video.google.com)
- AOL Video (http://video.aol.com)
- Yahoo! Video (http://video.yahoo.com)
- PutFile (www.putfile.com)
- VidiLife (www.vidilife.com)

By analyzing exactly what the competition does, you can always find ways to improve or exploit a competitor's actions. Best of all, knowing how to undercut a competitor means you'll also know how to defend your own business when a competitor tries to exploit your weaknesses—but only if you study your own business and your competition first.

The more you understand what you do and what the competition does, the better you'll be able to enhance your capabilities while weakening the competition.

How

The "how" of competitive intelligence asks, how does the competition work? How do they get customers and how do they treat them? How are they different from you? Knowing what competitors do is important, but knowing how they do it is crucial. If a competitor advertises through a web site, find out how he or she does it and then see if you could position your web site to appear first in search engine listings ahead of your competition.

Right now, take out a pencil and answer the following:

- Who are your primary competitors?
- Who are their customers?
- Who are your indirect competitors?
- What do your competitors offer that you don't?
- What are the biggest threats your competitors pose?
- What strategies are your competitors pursuing?
- What are the strengths and weaknesses of your competitors?
- What is their sales volume?
- What advertising methods do they use?
- What is their greatest competitive advantage?
- How does your competitor attract and treat customers?
- How does your competitor compete with you?
- How do people see your competitor?
- How do your competitors differ from you?
- How do your products or service compare to the competition?

Your Unique Selling Proposition (USP)

Every successful business needs a unique selling proposition (USP), which uniquely brands your business in the eyes of your customers.

Such a USP is crucial because it advertises your main advantage over the competition in a way that automatically eliminates them from your market.

For example, if you need to send a package overnight, what's the first name that comes to mind? Federal Express (FedEx), but not the post office or even United Parcel Service (UPS), both of which also offer overnight delivery, often at a lower rate. Federal Express branded its USP in the minds of consumers better than any of its competitors through one simple statement in its marketing messages: "Federal Express: When it absolutely, positively has to be there overnight."

That USP makes it easy for customers to understand. Need overnight service? Think Federal Express.

Another famous USP that allowed a pizza company to become one of the largest and most successful franchises in history belongs to Domino's Pizza. Despite having literally thousands of local competitors all across the country, Domino's dominated the market because of one simple USP: "Hot, fresh pizza delivered in 30 minutes or less, guaranteed."

Leaders in every business have a USP that in many cases has been embedded in the public's perception for so long that people automatically think of a certain company when they need a particular product or service. There are plenty of competitors who offer identical service or products, but each company's USP literally channels your thinking away from the competition and straight to them. That's the power of a USP and that's why you need one for your business. A great USP becomes indirect advertising that forever sticks in your customers' heads.

For your business, ask what's the most prominent, positive feature or service your business can offer and that your competition either can't or hasn't done? Your USP needs to highlight the main reason customers should do business with you and ideally separate you from the competition. Make your USP short, simple, and positive.

Ideally, your USP should play to your strength and your passion. You want your USP to be something that's easy for you to do while being hard for your competitors to imitate. For example, suppose you had a choice of taking your car to be fixed at two repair shops. The first repair shop is a typical one with no USP.

Now consider a second repair shop that promises a 90-day quality guarantee or your money back. Assuming the price is roughly the same, would you want to go to an ordinary repair shop or one with a USP of guaranteed service?

As you can see, it's not difficult to create a unique USP that makes doing business with you much more attractive than your competitors. And lucky for you, most companies simply don't utilize this strategy, which makes your job that much easier.

The three main types of USPs are:

- Speed
- Quality
- Price

Federal Express, Domino's Pizza, Jiffy Lube, and other companies all emphasize speed as their USP. Other companies, like Apple, Nordstrom, Lexus, and Craftsman Tools, all emphasize quality. Wal-Mart, Costco, and McDonald's emphasize low prices.

Ask yourself in which area your business can thrive. From your short list of possible USPs, ask yourself which one would be the easiest for you to sustain without a doubt and that will be your USP.

Warning! I realized in business long ago that you cannot focus on all three. When you try to be all things to all people, you end up watering down your USP. Focus on one of the three to be your core USP.

You want a USP that's easy to implement, attainable, and believable. Once you discover your USP, the final step is to make sure you constantly advertise and promote your USP until it's embedded in your customers' heads. Now when your customers think of a product or service in your industry, they'll think of you first, and that will put you miles ahead of the competition no matter what else they might do.

Here's a simple formula to help you get started identifying your USP. Basically, you just need to fill in four blanks to determine the focus of your business:

(Business name) is a (business category) that helps (core audience) achieve (key benefit).

Here are some examples:

FedEx is a package delivery service that helps people and businesses send packages overnight.

Wal-Mart is a department store that helps people save money on everyday items.

Craftsman is a tool company that helps people buy high-quality tools that come with a lifetime guarantee.

Plug in your own business name and category, and see what type of USP you can create for your own business.

10

The Ultimate Time-Leveraging Business

Wealth, like happiness, is never attained when sought after directly. It comes as a byproduct of providing a useful service.

—Henry Ford

If you have a job, this is what I want you to do. Go into work tomorrow and tell your boss that you want to work for the next ten years and then you want to stop. However, after you stop working, you still want your boss to keep paying you the exact same yearly income or more for the rest of your life.

What kind of a reaction will you get? I think you know the answer. If you work in any job for ten years and stop, your income stops at that moment, too. However, the average person who spends ten years working in a particular network marketing company earns a full-time income on a residual basis, meaning he or she could completely stop working and would still have that income coming in.

If you've never heard of network marketing (also called multilevel marketing, word of mouth marketing, referral marketing, or direct selling), this is how it works.

Ask yourself how many times you've seen a great movie and then told your friends about it. If your friends then go to see that movie, how much does the theater pay you? If you guessed nothing, you would be right. And what about when your friends go tell their friends who then go see the movie? Do you earn anything from that? Once again, the answer is no.

Now imagine a business that pays you a referral commission to send friends or even strangers to purchase products from a company. Then when your referrals in turn refer others (your second generation of referrals), you get paid commissions as well. When that second generation refers the third, the third refers the fourth, the fourth refers the fifth, and so on, you get paid commissions on the sales generated from everyone. That's the basis of network marketing.

Most traditional companies spend money to advertise on TV, radio, magazines, or newspapers. When customers show up, the company keeps all the revenues for itself and uses part of those funds to do more advertising and attract more customers.

Network marketing companies rarely do any advertising at all, which allows them to save money. Instead, network marketing companies rely on their customers or independent representatives to advertise the company and its products. Each time a representative refers someone who buys something from the company, the network marketing company pays that person a commission. The more customers you bring to a company, the more money you make, thereby encouraging you to keep sending the company even more customers.

The company benefits because instead of spending money on advertising, the company spends it on paying commissions to its sales representatives. Since one of the most effective forms of marketing is word of mouth, network marketing companies actually save money by not advertising and just relying on happy customers telling others about the company's products.

Many people have a negative reaction toward network marketing, whether from past experience or exposure. Unfortunately, there have been a number of network marketing companies over the years that have used misleading business practices such as inviting people to meetings under false pretenses, selling overpriced products, and promising pie-in-the sky incomes for little to no effort. While those companies have left a sour taste in the mouth of many consumers, there are hundreds of legitimate network marketing companies that have wonderful products and operate in complete integrity. However you may feel, the truth is that network marketing offers one of the most lucrative business models available today.

If you have any doubts about network marketing as a viable business, perhaps you'd like to know what one of the wealthiest men on the planet, Donald Trump, has to say: "Network marketing has proven itself to be a viable and rewarding source of income, and the challenges could be just right for you. There have been some remarkable examples of success, and those successes have been earned through diligence, enthusiasm and the right product combined with timing. As with so many issues, there are tangibles and intangibles involved, but success is not a total mystery, and that applies to network marketing, as well."[1]

Robert Kiyosaki, the best-selling author of *Rich Dad, Poor Dad*, says: "Many network marketing companies are really business schools that teach values not found in traditional business schools . . . values such as the best way to become rich is to teach yourself and other people to become business owners, rather than teach them to be a loyal employee working for the rich."[2]

If two of the most successful businesspeople in the country endorse network marketing, shouldn't you at least look into it for yourself?

After getting laid off from a corporate job, I decided to join a network marketing company. I worked my tail off for six months, which allowed me to create a six-figure income. Because of residual income, I was able to take as much time off as I wanted, to the point where I took seven different vacations in five and a half months.

---

[1] *SUCCESS* Magazine, April/May 2008.
[2] Ibid.

Success in network marketing is both an art and a science. In fact, one of my next books will be a complete "no holds barred" book on how you can apply specific and proven principles to succeed in network marketing. Check my web site, www.MattMorris.com, for details on when this book will become available.

Dealing with Today's Economic Crisis

Before I talk about network marketing and the rest of the Unemployed Millionaire models that you can follow, let's discuss the current worldwide economic crisis, which is the worst since the Great Depression. Millions of jobs have been lost, home values are the lowest they've been in decades, stock markets have plummeted to the lowest levels in almost 20 years, and consumer confidence is at an all-time low. It seems that everywhere you look, the forecast for the near future is gloom and doom.

In light of these negative messages that you're bombarded with on television, radio, and print media, I'd like to shed some light on one of your greatest opportunities to profit.

You may have heard that the Chinese symbol for "crisis" is actually made up of two characters. One represents danger and the other represents opportunity.

The wealthy of the world realize that during this economic "crisis" there is an even greater "opportunity" for those who choose their business endeavors wisely.

There are two facts I'd like to share with you, not only to recession-proof your mind-set, but to give you an even greater optimism than ever before.

The first fact is simply realizing that there is not any less amount of *money* during a recession than there is during an economic boom. In fact, in the United States, our government is printing more money to help stimulate the economy. Let's face it; it's not as if billions of dollars have simply vanished, been burned, or dropped to the bottom of the ocean. Those billions have simply been taken from the hands of many and been reappropriated into the hands of the few.

So the question that begs an answer is this: How do *you* become "the few"? This leads me to the second fact, which should give you more excitement about network marketing once you better understand its history.

In the late 1950s, unemployment was at its highest since the Great Depression. This was the time that network marketing began to flourish with the opening of such pioneering companies as Shaklee and Amway.

This continued into the early 1960s with companies such as Mary Kay, Avon, Tupperware, and Fuller Brush all gaining momentum.

Again, during the 1980s we saw the network marketing industry really flourish in the first half of the decade when the unemployment rate reached 9.7 percent, its highest level in 40 years.

This cycle continued in the 1990s when the network marketing industry experienced huge momentum. In fact, "there was more wealth created in by way of MLM from 1990 to 1994 than any other time in history."[3] Again, in direct correlation to unemployment levels.

As you can see, the network marketing industry has an inverse relationship to the economy. During economic downtrends, network marketing typically booms.

So if you're serious about network marketing, believe it or not, a recession could be the best thing that's ever happened to your financial future. Shaky economic times produce a renewed awareness of the need to make more money. You'll find that people who were previously uninterested in network marketing are suddenly looking for new financial opportunities. They want a business that doesn't require a lot of capital, allows them to establish their own hours, and offers financial rewards greater and more stable than they can receive through a job. More people than ever are looking for a plan B.

So rather than follow what I call the "herd" mentality of being overly pessimistic, my recommendation is to take a serious look at network marketing as one of your greatest opportunities for growth and success based on proven economic trends.

---

[3] *Network Marketing Lifestyles*, May 2000.

Network Marketing Basics

There are two basic ways to make money in any network marketing company:

- Sell products yourself.
- Sell products *and* build a sales organization.

By only selling products yourself, you earn a decent income through regular and consistent sales. Of course, if you stop selling products, you stop earning income, so the second, and far more lucrative, way to make money in network marketing is to also build a sales organization.

As a general rule in any business, the more time you put into a business, the greater your results. So if you put in 10 hours of work, you'll generally get 10 hours of results.

Now if you enroll one person in your sales organization and you each put in 10 hours worth of work, you'll get 20 hours worth of results. If each of you enrolls just one more person, you'll now have four people in your sales organization and you'll be producing 40 hours worth of results, yet you'll still only be putting in 10 hours worth of work yourself. Take a look at Table 10.1 to see how this multiplying effort can continue to grow.

TABLE 10.1   Comparison of Effort vs. Results

Number of people in your sales organization	Hours of work you put into the business	Hours of results you receive
1	10	10
2	10	20
4	10	40
8	10	80
16	10	160
32	10	320
64	10	640
128	10	1,280
256	10	2,560
512	10	5,120

As you can see, you only need to keep putting forth the same number of hours yourself; but if you keep growing your sales organization, the results you get keeps growing exponentially.

The Planting Season

The key to network marketing is getting started, which is what I call the planting season. Just as in farming, the planting season is when you work very hard and see little or no results. Think of a farmer who plows a field, plants seed, waters the crops, and initially sees nothing but mounds of dirt for his efforts.

These are the same type of results you'll typically get from network marketing initially, and this is the time when most people give up. Most people still have a job mentality where they trade hours for dollars. They want to receive money for each hour they work. If they put in 10 hours in a network marketing business, they get discouraged if they don't immediately see 10 hours worth of results. For most people, putting in 10 hours worth of work with no guarantee of seeing any pay in return is simply absurd.

What's great though, for those who stick it out, is that eventually, when exponential growth kicks in, you end up working the same amount, or even less, yet receive huge results in return. When I was 24 years old, I started working with a network marketing company and saw very little income in return. Less than six months later, I was still working just the same, yet I was now earning approximately $10,000 each week.

The key to network marketing is to put forth a lot of effort initially and reap the rewards later in the future. At the beginning, you put in a lot of time for insignificant results. Then after steady and consistent work, you'll find that this model flips upside down and you suddenly start earning a huge income for the same amount or even less time. To succeed in any network marketing business, you must be willing to go through this initial learning phase.

Some people, such as my good friend Johnny Wimbrey, make $100,000 in their first four months in the network marketing industry. While it's rare for someone to make that much money in such a short amount of time, it's not impossible. What is impossible is to make that same amount of money in such a short time working in practically any *job* in the world.

To succeed in any network marketing business, you must treat it like a business and you'll get paid like a business. Treat it as a hobby and it will pay like a hobby.

What makes network marketing so appealing is its low-cost of entry. To get started, you'll typically spend anywhere from $200 to $2,000, which makes network marketing one of the easiest businesses to start. If you wanted to open a McDonald's restaurant or an Exxon gas station, you'd need $1 million just to pay for franchise fees, put up the building, buy supplies, and hire employees, not to mention the constant headache of managing your whole business every day.

With network marketing, anyone can get started regardless of your background or experience. Can you imagine having no experience or education and applying for a job as a brain surgeon? For many people, the best paying jobs are beyond their reach until they complete the necessary education and training experience. In network marketing, everyone is welcome. Obviously, some people will always be better suited than others due to previous background or experience, but anyone with enough desire and determination can succeed in network marketing. After all, I dropped out of college and only had a high school diploma, yet by age 25 I was earning a six-figure income. If I hadn't been in network marketing, I may never have been able to earn a six-figure income in any job. The income I earned through network marketing allowed me the small start-up capital to start my own Internet marketing business that catapulted my income.

One of the greatest aspects of involvement in network marketing is that the network marketing company handles all the accounting, product fulfillment, and logistics of running your business. All you have to do is promote the company and its products.

Easy in, Easy out

Of course, the ease of getting into network marketing also makes it much easier to leave. If you only spent $300 to start your network marketing business, you have much less at stake than if you had invested one million to start a McDonald's franchise. Nobody would sink one million into a business and then give up six months later if it didn't seem to be working like they expected.

Unfortunately, beginners in network marketing too often give up because their initial investment is so low, so here's the trick I use. When I got involved in network marketing, I had the mind-set that I had just invested $1 million. That mind-set gave me the determination to succeed no matter what obstacles popped up.

Because network marketing is about meeting new people and working with your sales organization, the biggest factor in network marketing success is to truly like people and to understand that all network marketing involves a learning phase.

Just like it takes a doctor or lawyer a few extra years of schooling, network marketing also requires a period of time where you'll need to learn the ropes. And just like with a doctor or lawyer, once you've been through the schooling—or in network marketing, what I call the planting season—you'll have the ability to earn a tremendous income with a lifestyle that is second to none. It will take time and effort, but as my own life clearly demonstrates, the rewards will be well worth it.

Finding a Network Marketing Company

Not every network marketing company is equal, and not everyone will have success in the same network marketing company. Every network marketing company sells different products and offers different compensation plans. That means you could have massive success in one company but only mediocre success in another one simply because of the products offered. Don't try to find the "hot" product that you think will be most successful. Look for the product that gets *you* most excited and that's the best product for *you*. The key to success in network marketing comes from keeping yourself excited and bought-in psychologically to the product you're selling.

Generally every network marketing company goes through four distinct phases:

- Formulation
- Concentration
- Momentum
- Stability

A company is first formed in the formulation stage. This is often the time everyone rushes to the company because it's new and thus offers products that many people have never seen before. That means there are fewer distributors and more opportunities for everyone. Such companies often begin with nothing and sky-rocket to millions in sales. While you may think this would be the best time to get into a particular network marketing company, be careful.

It's an unfortunate fact, but 90 to 95 percent of all businesses fail within the first two years, and network marketing is no exception. That means for every ten network marketing companies that start up, only one will last beyond two years. With a 10 percent chance of finding a company that will survive, but a 90 percent chance of getting stuck with a company that goes bankrupt, the odds of success are against you.

If you're lucky enough to find one out of ten companies that survives past two years, you could experience quick success if you put in a lot of work. However, there's a much better chance that you'll end up part of a company that goes out of business, which will require you to start all over again.

If you get involved with another network marketing company, most, if not all, of your current sales organization will *not* follow you into another company, which means you'll essentially be starting from scratch. Sure, you'll have gained some experience, but having to start from scratch each time is not the ideal situation for building long-term, residual income.

Companies survive their initial growth phase without growing their expenses faster than their income in the concentration stage. This is the time when a company fine-tunes its branding, product messaging, and marketing systems and develops a core group of successful field leadership. If a network marketing company makes it through this phase and properly prepares its infrastructure, it will likely be poised for momentum.

Many people can achieve massive success in a short time during the momentum stage. This typically happens anywhere from around $50 to $100 million in annual sales. During the momentum stage, the company has established its foundation for growth so that a flood of new orders and distributors won't overwhelm it. The momentum stage is when companies begin to experience exponential growth and is typically the time when the multimillion-dollar earners are produced. During, or just before, this phase is the optimum time to get into a network marketing company.

After spiraling growth, network marketing companies fall into the stability stage, where they experience slow growth (such as 5 to 10 percent a year, in comparison to doubling, tripling, or quadrupling during the momentum stage). Older, well-established companies fall into this category. Oftentimes companies in the stability stage can only repeat their initial growth and success of the momentum stage by expanding into foreign markets.

If you find two identical companies and product lines, but one company is cruising in stability mode while the other is starting its momentum stage, you'll probably achieve much greater success going with the company in momentum.

While the best time to join any network marketing company is before or during its momentum stage, people can achieve success with a network marketing company in any stage of its growth. What's more important than the age of the company is your own passion for that company's products and belief in the company itself.

If you don't care about a particular product, it won't matter if the company is tripling its sales every month since you won't be an effective representative. Likewise, it doesn't matter if a company is stuck in the stability stage and growing slowly. If you love its products and trust the company, you'll have far greater success than in a much younger company simply because your passion will help you build your sales organization faster and easier.

Mistakes to Avoid

The biggest mistake many people make is switching from one company to another, trying to find the one "hot" new network marketing company. Remember, each time you switch to a different network marketing company, you'll lose most of the sales organization you've painstakingly built up and you'll have lost some of your credibility as a businessperson. The key to network marketing is building a large sales organization once over time, not in finding the "hot" network marketing company.

The next mistake that people make is signing up with two or more network marketing companies under the idea that at least one of these companies will become "hot" and make them a fortune.

In my 15 years of experience, I have never seen anyone successfully run two or more network marketing businesses at the same time. I like to say that you can only ride one horse at a time. If you divide your attention between multiple companies, chances are you'll end up failing in both.

Success in network marketing comes from persistence and determination building one large sales organization. A single team working under the same company will always generate more momentum than scattered efforts diluted between multiple companies. As a general rule, find one network marketing company and stick with it.

What to Look For

Aside from finding a company that sells products you can believe in and get passionate about, look for a company with leadership that exhibits complete integrity. I was once involved in a network marketing company where I made a six-figure income, but I chose to walk away from it because I lost faith in the company's leadership when they seemed more interested in making money than in doing the right thing. By no surprise, the company was out of business a few months later. The bedrock of success for any network marketing company is its foundation of integrity. In addition, when you promote a company, that company's reputation and integrity will be a direct reflection of your reputation and integrity.

The number one question I've found that people have when looking to join a network marketing company is, "Can I do it?" Most people are not trained in sales, so if they have to do all the selling themselves, their chances of success will be slim. This is why it's important to look for a network marketing company that already has a strong sales and marketing program. If the company provides presentation tools to do the selling, all you and your organization have to do is use these tools to do the presenting for you. Examples of presenting tools might include CDs, DVDs, brochures, magazines, conference calls, or web sites—anything that can assist you in selling the company and its products. The more sophisticated the company's sales tools, the easier it will be for you to promote.

Next, I'd immediately look for a mentor in that network marketing company. A mentor should have a track record of success not just in building his or her own income, but in assisting others in creating success as well. Successful mentors in network marketing come from all walks of life and all different backgrounds. You and your mentor may have completely different personality styles and in some cases you may not even like them very much. In fact, I was having dinner a few months ago with a friend of mine who has earned over 50 million dollars in the last 20 years. He was telling me that he hasn't even had dinner with his mentor in as many years because he doesn't consider his mentor a friend even though he talks with him regularly and gives his mentor credit for his success. Above all else, your mentor must be someone you trust and believe in.

I still remember the moment I met my mentor in network marketing. The first time I met him, I knew I wanted him to mentor me because immediately after seeing an opportunity presentation, he began to train and educate me on what it takes to be successful even *before* I joined the company. Sure, he was exciting and a great salesperson, but I could tell he was genuinely interested in *my* success, not just his own.

When looking for a mentor, definitely avoid dealing with anyone who only talks about the money you can make. These people will tell you it will be easy to earn quick riches just to get you to sign up, which sets up false expectations. You *can* earn a tremendous income and there's nothing wrong with a leader telling you so, but if money is their master, they are not the leader you want to emulate.

I've generated millions of dollars inside network marketing by being a representative as well as owning my own network marketing company. I've also generated millions of dollars outside of network marketing through Internet marketing and have to admit that the best lifestyle with the least amount of stress I've ever had was working as a representative in network marketing.

Although I've personally achieved tremendous financial success through network marketing, and I truly believe anyone can achieve similar or even greater results as well, network marketing isn't the only way to become an Unemployed Millionaire. In the next chapters, I'll explain other business models that can also offer you the lifestyle of an Unemployed Millionaire.

Internet Marketing

Try not to become a man of success but rather to become a man of value.

—Albert Einstein

In the old days if you wanted to start a business, you had to rent space and open a store. Since this was expensive and tied you to a physical location much like a job, some people found a way to escape this trap by running mail-order businesses from their home. The advantage of mail-order is that it frees you from being stuck to a specific location. While you must still be tied to a post office box, you can choose to set up business anywhere and move any time you wish.

Over the last decade, the trend for direct marketers has moved from mail-order to the Internet. Like mail-order, your customers aren't limited to a geographical area, but can literally be anywhere in the world. Unlike mail-order, which typically requires a very large budget for printing and postage, Internet marketing allows you to reach far more people at a fraction of the cost through

TABLE 11.1   How to Earn $1,000,000

Cost of Product (US$)	Number needed sold	% of Internet users
1	1,000,000	.067
10	100,000	.0067
50	20,000	.0013
100	10,000	.00067
200	5,000	.0003
300	3,334	.0002
400	2,500	.00016
500	2,000	.00013
1,000	1,000	.00006

e-mail and other forms of digital advertising. Rather than printing expensive color catalogs, you can design a web site that you can update in seconds and host on the Internet for a minimal charge. The Internet has leveled the playing field on a greater scale than any other marketing platform in our history. So much so that any business not on the Internet is almost not considered a business at all.

With over 1.5 billion Internet users worldwide,[1] Internet marketing is one of the easiest ways to become an Unemployed Millionaire. Let's say you have a product that you sell for $50. If you sell just 20,000 of them, you'll make a million dollars. Reaching 20,000 customers might seem like a lot, but it's actually just a tiny fraction of the entire Internet population. (See Table 11.1)

If you're selling products that cost more than $50, you can still become a millionaire by selling to even fewer customers. Take a look at Table 11.1 to see how many products you'll need to sell in a year to make a million dollars and what percentage of Internet users you'll need to reach. With a billion-and-a-half users on the Internet and more coming online every day, earning a million dollars online is well within reach.

With many brick and mortar businesses, you need to buy and stock inventory. With Internet marketing, you have the option of

---

[1]Internet World Stats.

shipping physical products like books, or digital products like e-books. Shipping digital products costs virtually nothing to store or ship, and also allows you to sell unlimited copies with no worries of running out of inventory. Even if you do ship physical products, you don't necessarily need to buy and hold inventory yourself. Instead, each time a customer orders a product, you can route that order to the manufacturer or a fulfillment house, which can send that product directly to the customer without you lifting a finger. Internet marketing offers the freedom of mail-order on a much larger scale.

Three popular ways to make money from the Internet, which we'll discuss in this chapter, include:

- Selling your own products
- Selling other people's products as an affiliate (Pay-per-performance)
- Displaying advertisements of other people's products (Pay-per-click)

The simplest way to make money on the Internet is to sell something. This may sound incredibly basic if you have experience online, but if you're the type of person who considers yourself a technical dunce, selling anything at all may be a challenge. If you're brand new to marketing online, don't worry about understanding everything right away. Realize that you'll need to crawl before you can walk, and walk before you can run.

How to Earn Your First Dollar Online in Less than a Week

The most important accomplishment for any new Internet entrepreneur is to simply earn your first dollar online. Once you've earned your first dollar, you'll have gotten past the biggest psychological barrier that stops most people and that's the mind-set that you *can* actually make money online. Once you've sold something, even if it's only for a few bucks, you'll realize that making money online isn't really as hard as you might think.

If you've never sold anything online, I'm going to show you how to quickly make your first dollar (okay, probably more than a dollar) online this week. The easiest way to accomplish that goal is to sell something through an online auction site.

Online Auctions

If you find something in your garage or closet, you might try to sell it through a yard or garage sale, or you might advertise it through the classified ads. The problem with both solutions is that you may not find anyone who wants to buy it, and if you do find someone who wants it, he or she may not want to pay as much as you hope the item is worth.

To avoid both problems, you can sell stuff online through auction sites. The idea is simple. You place an item up for sale, display a picture of that item with a short description, and wait until people bid on it. After a fixed amount of time, such as two weeks, you sell your item to the highest bidder. Each time you sell an item, the auction site typically takes a percentage of the sale, such as 1.5 percent.

Online auctions solve two problems at once. First, an online auction is open to anyone in the world so you can reach the widest audience possible for your item. Second, an online auction typically attracts motivated buyers who specifically want what you're selling. As a result, auction buyers often bid a price far higher than you might get if you had just sold that same item through a garage sale in front of your house.

Selling products through an online auction is probably the easiest way to make money on the Internet because everyone can find something in their garage, bedroom, or closet that they no longer need or want. Rather than throw it away or donate it, sell it online. With the whole world available as potential customers, there's a good chance someone will want what you have and be willing to pay a nice price to get it.

Even if you run out of your own stuff to sell, you can easily pick up other items from flea markets, garage sales, and used bookstores, and sell them online. One time I bought a book through an online auction site and ended up needing to talk to the seller because the book didn't get delivered. She quickly refunded my money and we ended up discussing her business. It turned out that she and her husband traveled around the country in a motor home and visited garage sales and cheap bookstores where they bought used books for, on average, one to two dollars each. Then they listed the books on auction web sites for anywhere from $5 to $15 and earned an extra few hundred dollars a month while having fun traveling.

Let's get you started by making money online right now. First, you have to find an online auction site. The most popular one is eBay (www.ebay.com), but there are plenty more to choose from:

- uBid (www.uBid.com)
- Bidz (www.bidz.com)
- Overstock (www.auctions.overstock.com)

Since eBay is the most popular one with the most buyers, let's start there. Just keep in mind that almost all online auction sites work pretty much the same.

First, find something around your house that you don't want or need anymore, but is too valuable to just throw away. This could be a book, an antique, an electronic device (such as a game console), or anything else that you know someone will value, such as a collectible of any kind. While you could try selling complete junk, you'll have much more success if you try selling something that you know someone else will find valuable.

Now, using a digital camera, take a picture of your item in the most flattering position possible. If you're selling a book, take a picture of the book cover, but consider tilting it slightly to show that the pages and the rest of the cover are in good condition. Your picture will be the only way someone can judge your product, so take time to get the best picture possible.

To advertise your item, you'll need to give it a title and a description. The title identifies the item (such as "Vintage 25 Cent Postage Stamp Machine"), while the description provides additional detail. For example, "The vending machine is made of maroon coated cast iron in fine condition. Very minimal paint chipping. The vending machine has a clear plastic rear housing with a

FULL BRASS ANTIQUE STYLE CANDLESTICK TELEPHONE

Bidder or seller of this item? Sign in for your status

Current bid:	**US $77.55**
Your maximum bid:	US $ [ ] [Place Bid >]
	(Enter US $78.55 or more)
End time:	**57 mins 40 secs** (Feb-28-09 22:17:00 PST)
Shipping:	**US $25.00** Standard Flat Rate Shipping Service Service to United States
Ships to:	Worldwide
Item location:	Townsville, Australia
History:	7 bids
High bidder:	s***y (3)
You can also:	(Watch This Item) Get SMS or IM alerts | Email to a friend

Listing and payment details: **Show**

Make no payments & pay no interest for 3 months with an eBay MasterCard. With no annual fee! US Residents Only. See Details \| Apply Now

FIGURE 11.1   An eBay Listing Displaying a Picture of a Product, a Price, and an Auction Deadline

screwed-in metal carry handle at top. It stands 13" tall, 6.5" wide, and 9" deep." Figure 11.1 shows a typical eBay listing.

Remember, your item description is also a sales pitch. You want to describe your item accurately, so potential buyers will know what they're getting, but you also want to get people excited about it, too. Focus on its advantages and potential benefits while minimizing, but being honest about, its flaws.

Some additional items you can specify is how you'll accept payment (such as credit card, check, PayPal, or money orders), whether you will pay for shipping and where you'll ship (such as only within the United States), a starting minimum bid, and a reserve price, which specifies the least amount you'll accept. If you don't state a reserve price, you may think your item is worth $100, but somebody might be the highest bidder at just $19.25.

Finally, you'll need to specify a category to place your item (such as Collectibles, Books, or Crafts) and how long you want your auction to last (such as 3, 7, or 10 days). Then get ready to start your auction and watch the bids come in. By the end of your auction, you'll have a winner, and you'll have to ship your item to the highest bidder.

Congratulations—You've just made your first dollar over the Internet!

Selling items on eBay is really as simple as that. Of course, to make significant money through auctions, you'll need more products than what you can find while cleaning out your garage or attic.

Basically, people buy stuff on auction sites for two reasons:

- They can't find those items anywhere else.
- The price is great.

If you're selling a rare guitar that Elvis Presley autographed, you'll find plenty of bidders. However, if you're just selling an ordinary guitar that anyone can buy from his or her neighborhood pawn shop, you better have a low enough price to make it worth getting.

Finding rare items to sell can take time, but you can always browse through local flea markets and garage sales. If you know about books, you'll be able to spot rare books or first editions and pick them up for bargain prices while selling them for a huge markup through eBay.

If you can't find rare items on a consistent basis, consider selling ordinary items at extraordinary prices. Some people sell socks and underwear because they can buy them in bulk at a low enough price to still make a profit and undercut local stores at the same time. One method is to buy products from a wholesaler and then ship those products out yourself. A second method is to use something called a drop-shipper.

The basic idea behind a drop-shipper is that you take the order, but the drop-shipper actually ships the product. The advantage is that you never have to worry about stocking products or shipping them out. The disadvantage is that you lose control over shipping. If you promised to send a package out within 24 hours, there's little you can do if your drop-shipper suddenly gets lazy and doesn't bother sending out the merchandise until three days later (or even worse, forgets to send the merchandise out at all). A second disadvantage of a drop-shipper is that the cost of hiring him or her also cuts into your profits, so you'll have to weigh the advantages of fewer hassles versus less income.

The advantage of storing and shipping products yourself is that you can control when you ship and can even insert "thank you" cards or other promotional materials inside the package. The disadvantage is that you need to buy and store inventory plus you have the hassle of packaging and mailing stuff, which can take away time to further market your business.

Before you buy any products to sell, check out the competition and find out if anybody is selling anything similar. If so, find out what price he or she wants for it. By knowing the typical price you can sell a product, you can avoid buying something that you can't sell for a profit online.

To increase sales and separate yourself from any competitors, consider bundling related items together, such as a piece of exercise equipment with a workout book or DVD. Such bundling gives your product added value, and if the added bonus doesn't cost much, the perceived value will likely attract a high enough bid that will cover the cost of the bonus item anyway.

Finally, focus on products that you care about. If you just try to sell something to make a fast buck, you probably won't be as successful as somebody who can not only describe an item, but can also chat about that same item with a degree of knowledge that a more disinterested seller could never do.

To find products that you can sell through auction sites, visit the following:

- Worldwide Brands (www.WorldwideBrandsStore.com): Highly recommended, as they give you access to thousands of products and they drop-ship for you. They are also an eBay Certified Solutions Provider and one of the most trusted and reliable wholesalers available.
- Ingram Micro (www.IngramMicro.com): Ingram Micro is the largest technology distributor in the world.

- Wholesale Central (www.wholesalecentral.com): One of the most comprehensive directories of current and active wholesalers.

- North American Wholesale Co-Op Association (www.nawca. org): Allows you access to over 2,000 wholesalers and over 1,000,000 products.

Remember, you don't have to be limited to a particular type of product such as clothes or electronics. Depending on what type of items you can buy, one week you might be selling shoes and the next week you might be selling low-cost DVDs. Unlike a regular store where you must sell the same type of products all the time, selling stuff through auctions gives you the freedom to sell whatever you can make the most profit on at the time.

Many people earn a part-time or even a full-time income selling stuff through online auction sites like eBay. As long as you have access to a computer, an Internet connection, and a way to ship your products to the highest bidder, you can literally run your online auction business from anywhere in the world while setting up your own working hours.

While some people are happy using online auction sites, most entrepreneurs who are earning tremendous profits online set up their own web site. By setting up your own web site, you'll have a much greater opportunity to expand your business through marketing and advertising, create joint venture partners, and even run an affiliate program to recruit others to market your products.

Creating Your Own Web Site

If you want to set up your own web site, you'll need to do the following:

- Reserve a domain name.
- Find a hosting company.
- Design your web pages.
- Set up a merchant account to process credit cards and other forms of payment such as PayPal.

If this sounds complicated or intimidating, trust me, it sounds harder than it really is, so let's walk through these steps one at a time.

Choosing a Domain Name

A domain name is how people can find your site on the Internet, such as www.amazon.com or www.ebay.com. Every domain name consists of two parts:

- The domain name
- A domain extension

The domain name typically contains the name of your business such as www.MattMorris.com or www.coca-cola.com. In the early days of the Internet, you could reserve descriptive one-word domain names like www.plumbing.com or www.shoes.com. However, most of these simpler domain names are no longer available.

If your business has a unique name, you can often reserve that domain name. So while www.hairstyling.com may already be taken, adding your own business name (such as www.marcieandjanehairstyling.com) may still be available.

If you haven't yet named your business, consider creating a unique spelling of your name since that name will likely be available. For example, instead of calling your business Quick Photos, you could name it Quik Photoz (www.quikphotoz.com). Creating unusual spellings often ensures that you can reserve your exact domain name, but unless people know your specific name, they may not know how to spell it correctly when searching for it over the Internet.

Another idea is to choose a domain name that describes your product or service. If you sell books, there's a good chance that domain names like www.books.com and www.rarebooks.com are already taken. However, there's less of a chance that www.summerbeachreadingmaterial.com is taken. Such a domain name may be longer to type, but ensures that you'll get the domain name that you want.

The second part of every domain name is the domain extension. The most popular extension is .com, which is short for "commercial" since the .com extension was meant to identify commercial enterprises.

When most people think of web site addresses, they almost always think of .com extensions, so most of the best domain names are already taken with the .com extension. To get around this problem, many businesses simply use a different extension.

One of the more popular extensions is .tv, which is especially suited for any business involved in video. Two other popular extensions are .net and .org. Just by changing the extension, you have an entirely different domain name. If someone has already reserved the domain name www.mybusiness.com, you might still be able to reserve the domain name www.mybusiness.net or www.mybusiness.org.

To find out if a particular domain name is available, you'll have to do a domain name search through one of the following:

- 1 and 1 Internet (www.1and1home.net)
- Network Solutions (www.networksolutions.com)

In case you need help coming up with a unique domain name, visit Name Boy (http://www.nameboy.com), which lets you type in different words. Then it shows you which domain names are already taken, along with variations of your chosen name that you might want to consider.

If you have your heart set on a particular domain name, visit one of the following web sites to purchase domain names that have already been registered, although usually at a much higher price tag:

- Sedo (www.sedo.com)
- Buy Domains (www.BuyDomains.com)
- Afternic (www.Afternic.com)

- Acquire This Name (www.AcquireThisName.com)
- Great Domains (www.GreatDomains.com)

Chances are good that popular domain names will fetch a hefty price tag, but less popular names will be much less expensive to reserve. You can also contact the owner of the web site to buy the domain if it's not in use. (Read Chapter 14, on joint ventures, to find out how to contact the web site owner.) I've purchased a number of great domain names for only a few hundred dollars, so don't be afraid to ask the owner to sell it to you.

Here's a secret about domain names. You can have more than one domain name and each domain name can point to the same web site. For example, one domain name might contain your business name, such as www.acmeplumbingsupplies.com, while the second domain name might describe your service, such as www.24hourplumbingservices.com. Pointing each domain name to the same web site effectively doubles your chances of capturing customers who are looking for your type of business. (I'll explain more about search engines later in this chapter.)

Reserving a domain name usually costs approximately $10 a year or less. When you reserve a domain name, you're paying for the right to use that name for your web site. Every domain name is unique, so it's important that you choose one that you like and that's easy for other people to find.

The only companies I use to register domains are:

- 1&1 (www.1and1home.net): The world's biggest and fastest growing web host. It is also the least expensive solution with exceptional service.
- GoDaddy (www.godaddy.com): My solution of choice before I found 1&1. Excellent service.

Reserving a domain name simply gives you the right to use that name. The second step is to host that domain name. Hosting simply means linking a web page to your domain name so other people can see your web page.

Once you reserve a domain name, you have to choose a hosting company. I'll give you some resources for that shortly, but for convenience, you can host your web site as an e-commerce site through a popular web site like Yahoo!

Creating an e-Commerce Store through a Third Party

The biggest problem with setting up any web site is that initially, nobody will know it even exists. To solve this problem of publicizing your site, some of the more popular web sites offer special e-commerce sites, specifically geared toward hosting online stores. Opening an e-commerce store on these web sites is like opening a store in a busy shopping mall. With so many people visiting every day, your chance of selling something increases significantly.

Besides taking advantage of the visitors that a popular web site already attracts, opening an e-commerce store on these web sites also has the advantage of simplicity. If you want to create your own web site, you have to do everything yourself: design your web pages, create online shopping carts, and set up a merchant account to accept credit card payments.

An e-commerce store eliminates many of those headaches (see Figure 11.2). The monthly fee to host your web site includes credit card processing and shopping cart software to let customers choose multiple products and order them. To set up an online store within another site, visit the following:

ores
ages.ebay.com/storefronts/seller-landing.html)
e by Amazon (http://webstore.amazon.com)
mall Business
nallbusiness.yahoo.com/ecommerce)
s (www.prostores.com)

	Starter Sign Up	Standard Sign Up	Professional Sign Up
Monthly price	$39.95/month	$129.95/month	$299.95/month
One-time setup fee	$50	$50	$50
Transaction fee	1.5%	1.0%	0.75%
Recommended plan if you expect sales of:	Less than $18K/mo.	$18K to $68K/mo.	More than $68K/mo.
Maximum number of products you can sell	50,000	50,000	50,000
Store Setup			
Third-party tools to build your store	✓	✓	✓
Upload product data	✓	✓	✓
Import an existing product database	✓	✓	✓
Customize checkout pages	✓	✓	✓
Product Promotion			
Cross-selling	⊖	✓	✓
Gift certificates	⊖	✓	✓
Affiliate Programs	✓	✓	✓
Payment and Order Processing			
Merchant Account for online credit card processing	✓	✓	✓
PayPal Express Checkout for online credit card processing	✓	✓	✓
Accept checks, money orders, PO's, COD's	✓	✓	✓

FIGURE 11.2 Some Features Available through an e-Commerce Site

Hosting your online store through a site like Amazon.com or eBay will cost you approximately $10 to $300 a month, depending on which web site you use.

Hosting and Building Your Own Web Site

While hosting an online store through a third party is an incredibly simple and easy way to get into business quickly, your options for growing and marketing your business will be a lot more limited than if you have your own web site. If you're looking to seriously grow your enterprise, you'll most certainly want the ability to control your own web site, to take advantage of a myriad of various marketing techniques.

The first two items to concern yourself with in owning your own web site are:

- Hosting your web site
- Creating/designing your web site

Many of the different web hosting companies offer very affordable pricing (as low as $3.99 a month and up), credit card processing, shopping cart software, chat rooms, forums, and templates that let you create web pages as easily as dragging and dropping pictures on a page and typing text.

Of course, you will likely have to pay additional credit card processing fees per transaction, and hosting your online store through these companies won't give you the built-in traffic that sites such as eBay or Amazon.com can attract.

Some of the more popular web hosting companies include:

- 1&1 (www.1and1home.net)
- Host Gator (www.hostgator.com)
- Fat Cow (www.fatcow.com)
- HostUpon (www.hostupon.com)
- Host Monster (www.hostmonster.com)

Hosting your web site will cost money, so you may be tempted to use a free web hosting services instead—don't. In exchange for hosting your web site, free services display advertisements on your web pages, which you can't control.

More importantly, free hosting services typically won't give you a unique domain name. Instead, you'll share the web hosting service's domain name. Instead of typing something simple like www.mycompany.com, you'll be forced to access your web site using a convoluted domain name like www.angelfire.com/184/mycompany. For personal web sites, a free web hosting service is fine, but not for running any type of business.

In creating a web site, you have three options:

- Create a web site from a template.
- Use a web page designing program.
- Hire a web page designer.

Creating a web site from a template basically contains the overall design of a web page, so all you have to do is plug in your own text and pictures. If your web hosting company doesn't provide any templates that you want to use, you can find templates on these sites:

- Template Monster (www.templatemonster.com)
- Website Templates (www.websitetemplates.com)
- Template World (www.templateworld.com)
- Templates Box (www.templatesbox.com)

If you want a little more flexibility and feel comfortable designing flyers or signs in a desktop publishing program, you may want to design your own web pages. For simple web pages this isn't hard, but unless you're an experienced web page designer, I would strongly advise against building the web site yourself.

Some popular web page creation programs include:

- Dreamweaver
  (www.adobe.com/products/dreamweaver)
- Nvu (www.net2.com/nvu)

- iWeb (www.apple.com/ilife/iweb)
- Microsoft Expression Web
  (www.microsoft.com/expression)
- RapidWeaver
  (www.realmacsoftware.com/rapidweaver)
- Contribute (www.adobe.com/products/contribute)

Nvu is completely free, so try this program first and see if you like designing your own web pages before spending money on a separate web page editor. Dreamweaver is one of the most expensive programs and the choice of most professional web designers. If you want absolute power in creating web pages (in exchange for greater complexity), you'll want Dreamweaver.

Both iWeb and RapidWeaver only run on the Macintosh while Microsoft Expression Web only runs on Windows, but all three are geared toward novices who want the flexibility of customizing a web site without the complexity.

If using a template seems too limiting and designing your own web pages too time-consuming, you can get the best of both worlds by hiring someone else to create a custom web site for you. Some sites where you can find and hire web page designers include:

- Elance (www.elance.com)
- Rent a Coder (www.RentaCoder.com)
- ScriptLance (www.ScriptLance.com)
- Affordable Programmers
  (www.AffordableProgrammers.com)
- Web Design Solutions
  (www.WebDesignOutsource.net)

These sites let both web designers and programmers advertise their services while also letting customers advertise their needs. Many of these sites link up freelancers who may live anywhere in the world, such as India or China. They generally charge a low price, but you may feel more comfortable finding a local web page designer whom you can meet and talk to periodically.

FIGURE 11.3   Shopping Cart Software Takes Care of the Details of Selling Online

If you're going to sell products on your web site, you'll need shopping cart software and a merchant account to process credit cards. Many of the web site hosting companies can provide you with shopping cart software and credit card processing, so you'll just need to inquire about this (see Figure 11.3).

In case your web hosting company doesn't offer shopping cart software or if you need enhanced functionality that is not available within their platform, you can link your web site to an outside shopping cart service. These services basically work by letting your web site display products and prices, and when an online shopper chooses something and pays for it, your web site directs the visitor to this other company's web site, which totals the amount and charges the credit card.

Some popular shopping cart software companies include:

- 1 Shopping Cart (www.1ShoppingCartSoftware.com)
- Volusion (www.volusion.com)
- Mal's e-Commerce (www.mals-e.com)
- 3d Cart (www.3dcart.com)

Every time you make a sale, the shopping cart company takes a percentage, in addition to any monthly fees. Shopping cart software takes the hassle out of selling products online while providing a secure and trusted way for customers to pay for your products.

Advertising Other People's Products

If you don't have anything of your own to sell, you can still make money on the Internet by advertising other people's products. Look at popular web sites like the Internet Movie Database (www.imdb.com), the Onion (www.theonion.com), or Fark (www.fark.com) and notice how many advertisements appear on the web page. Like TV networks that offer free shows in return for running commercials, web sites commonly offer free information in return for displaying advertisements on their web pages. The more popular your web site, the more lucrative advertising can be.

The two most popular advertising models are pay-per-click (PPC) and pay-per-performance (PPP). The pay-per-click model means you create a web site, display ads on your web pages, and every time someone clicks on one of your ads, you get paid a small amount.

Pay-per-performance, also known as affiliate marketing, only pays you if someone clicks on an ad and then buys something from that merchant. Depending on the merchant, you can get paid anywhere from 10 to 75 percent of the purchase price.

Many Internet marketers use both tactics of pay-per-click and pay-per-performance. The best example in the pay-per-click model is Google AdSense (www.google.com/adsense). The basic idea is that you sign up for a free account and define the type of ads you want to display on your web site, such as the size of the ads, the colors used to display the ads, and even the type of ads you don't want to appear (to block competitor's ads from appearing on your web site), as shown in Figure 11.4.

Text Ads

Leaderboard (728 x 90) - View sample placements

Cheap hotels	Save on Las Vegas Hotels	Devon PA Hotel Deals	Beach Hotels in Menorca
Find Hotels By Price, Star Rating Or Location. Cheap hotels www.ResortGateway.com	Amazing Las Vegas hotel discounts. Easily book your room today. www.Tripres.com	Shop and Compare Great Deals on Hotels in Devon PA. www.priceline.com	Deals on Menorca Beach Hotels. 1000's of Deals to Book Online! www.UlookUbook.com

Ads by Google

Banner (468 x 60) - View sample placements

Cheap hotels	Save on Las Vegas Hotels
Find Hotels By Price, Star Rating Or Location. Cheap hotels	Amazing Las Vegas hotel discounts. Easily book your room today.

Ads by Google

Button (125x125)

Cheap hotels
Find Hotels By Price, Star Rating Or Location. Cheap hotels
www.ResortGateway.com

Ads by Google

Half Banner (234x60)

Cheap hotels
Find Hotels By Price, Star Rating Or Location. Cheap hotels

Ads by Google

Skyscraper (120x600) - View sample placements

Ads by Google

Free Cheddar Chesse
4.4 lbs Of English Cheddar Cheese. Shipping Included. Act Now!
Food-Offer.com

Vermont Cheese
Made Fresh and Aged Slowly for a Great Taste. Variety of Types!
www.vermontcountrystc

Lost Garlic Bread Secret.
A long, lost Italian recipe for marvelous old country garlic bread.

Wide Skyscraper (160x600) - View sample placements

Ads by Google

Free Cheddar Chesse
4.4 lbs Of English Cheddar Cheese. Shipping Included. Act Now!
Food-Offer.com

Vermont Cheese
Made Fresh and Aged Slowly for a Great Taste. Variety of Types!
www.vermontcountrystore.com

Lost Garlic Bread Secret.
A long, lost Italian recipe for marvelous old country garlic bread.
www.GarlicValleyFarms.com

Cheese Info
Get Info on Cheese from 14 search engines in 1.

FIGURE 11.4 Google AdSense Lets You Define the Size of Ads to Appear on Your Web Site

To start making money through pay-per-click advertising, you'll need to sign up for a free account with one of the following programs:

- Google AdSense (www.google.com/adsense)
- Microsoft adCenter (adcenter.microsoft.com)
- LookSmart (www.looksmart.com)
- Chitika (https://chitika.com)

Affiliate Marketing

Pay-per-performance marketing, more commonly known as affiliate marketing, allows you to send traffic to a web site and earn commissions on any products sold. Affiliate marketing is great for beginners because you don't have to worry about product creation, web site design, fulfillment, credit card processing, and so forth. I've seen countless entrepreneurs with little to no experience start out as an affiliate until they learn how to successfully market online. Once they become successful as an affiliate, they then create their own products and take their success to greater heights.

To get started in affiliate marketing, you need to find one or more companies that offer affiliate programs. Rather than run their affiliate programs themselves, most companies use the services of an affiliate marketing company, which takes care of all the tracking of ads so companies know who sent them a customer, who needs to get paid, and how much they need to get.

One of the best ways to find products to market as an affiliate is through what's called an affiliate network, often referred to as a CPA (cost per acquisition/action) network. An affiliate network links sellers, which they typically call publishers, with affiliates, which they typically call advertisers.

These affiliate networks can also be a great resource for you to sell your products through affiliates should you decide to start marketing your own products.

Some popular affiliate/CPA networks include:

- ClickBank (www.clickbank.com): Over 10,000 products to choose from. My top recommendation for selling information products.
- Commission Junction (www.cj.com): Quite possibly the largest affiliate network online with many Fortune 500 companies as publishers.
- LinkShare (www.linkshare.com).
- ROI Rocket (www.roirocket.com).
- ShareASale (www.shareasale.com).
- Plimus (http://home.plimus.com).
- Azoogle (www.azoogleads.com).
- Market Leverage (www.marketleverage.com).
- Affiliate Tips (www.affiliatetips.com).
- Never Blue (www.neverblue.com).

Displaying Ads on a Web Site

Any web site can display ads. However, the only way you're going to get money through affiliate programs is if you can get enough people to click on your web site's ads, and the only way to get people to click on ads is to get people to your web site.

Just putting up a web site is like putting up a billboard in the middle of Death Valley. If nobody knows where to find it, nobody will ever see it. So the biggest task of any web site is to drive visitors or traffic to that site.

One of the more common ways to attract visitors is to provide some type of information/education/entertainment. This can range from simple advice on how to fix common problems in a house (how to fix a leaky faucet), displaying humorous stories or satirical news, or showing unusual information from around the world. Some popular content-oriented sites include:

- www.break.com: A humor site aimed at men.
- www.fark.com: A collection of bizarre news stories from around the world.

- www.theonion.com: A satirical news site.
- www.lifehacker.com: A collection of tips for doing things yourself, from brewing your own beer to editing photos on your computer.

Content-oriented sites rely on information to attract visitors. Online stores are simply sites that sell products, although online stores often provide both information and products for sale. Since people already have a reason to visit an online store, displaying ads (from noncompeting businesses) provides an additional source of revenue. Visit a site such as Amazon.com and you'll even see advertisements for products that Amazon.com doesn't sell.

By far the most common web sites are those that offer content, typically generated by the web site owner. The most common type of content sites are blogs, which act like online diaries where anyone can jot down his or her thoughts about a particular topic and attract readers. To see some of the more popular blogs, visit the following:

- Boing, Boing (www.boingboing.net): Covers interesting and unusual items.
- BloggingStocks (www.bloggingstocks.com): Covers the financial markets.
- Gizmodo (http://gizmodo.com): Covers interesting gadgets.

While some sites are strictly blogs, remember that you can include a blog on any site. For example, you might have your main web site that sells your products and then have a blog that covers your latest thoughts concerning your business and industry.

Whether you're marketing your own products, or other people's products as an affiliate, the key is attracting people to the web site. Some common traffic generation techniques are:

- Search engine optimization
- Signature files
- Article marketing
- E-mail newsletters
- Pay-per-click advertising

- Ezine advertising
- Face-to-face networking
- Recruiting affiliates and joint venture partners to market your web site

Search Engine Optimization

When people look for information on the Internet, they inevitably turn to a search engine such as Yahoo! or Google. Since search engines can direct people to your web site, the easiest way to get listed in a search engine is to submit your web site's address directly to the search engine. If you don't submit your site to a search engine, the search engines will probably find your web site eventually since they have computer programs that do nothing but crawl around the Internet looking for new web sites. However, the simple act of submitting your web site to a search engine can make those search engines find your site much faster.

Although you can hire the services of a company that will submit your site to multiple search engines, you can also do it yourself. Since there are only a handful of important search engines, you'll only need to visit one or more of the following to start getting your site listed:

- Google (www.google.com/submityourcontent)
- Yahoo! (http://au.siteexplorer.search.yahoo.com/free/submit)
- MSN Live Search (http://search.live.com/docs/submit.aspx)
- Open Directory Project (www.dmoz.org/add.html)

Getting your site listed on a search engine is easy, but getting your site listed near the top of a search engine's list isn't quite as easy. Usually when somebody searches for a word or phrase through a search engine, they look at the first one or two pages of results and stop right there. To get your site listed first, or as close to first as possible, requires something called search engine optimization (SEO).

Since all search engines use a complex algorithm to determine which sites appear first in a search, the main idea behind SEO is to fill your web site with the common keywords that someone might use to find your site. For example, if you run a seafood restaurant, people might try to find a good seafood restaurant in their area by typing in terms such as "seafood," "restaurant," or "seafood restaurant Dallas" into a search engine.

When you're creating a web site, think of the most likely keywords someone might use to find your site and be sure the word shows up at least a few times on your web site. You'll also want to make sure the most highly searched keywords are listed in the "meta tags" of your web site for your web site description, keywords, and ideally your title.

If this last sentence sounds Greek, don't worry, any programmer should know how to do this for you. Basically, every web page consists of a title (which appears in the top of your browser window) and meta tags (which are used to identify the type of information stored on your web page). Both the title and meta tags are used by search engines to identify and find your web site.

To see a web page's title and meta tags, go to www.google.com and type in "learn to play guitar." Now choose the first organic listing that pulls up. (An organic listing is one that is not a paid ad.) The site that pulls up as of the writing of this book is www.GuitarPlayerWorld.com.

From your browser, click "Edit" (or "View") → "Page Source." You can see at the very top the title, which looks like this:

Learn How to Play Guitar | Learn Guitar | Free Guitar Lessons

Notice how the title is packed with highly searched keywords. You'll also see the meta description and keywords: <meta NAME = "keywords," and <meta NAME = "description," which also include "learn how to play guitar." This site is a perfect example of how to use keywords in your web site code for SEO (see Figure 11.5).

Once you've selected a list of keywords and you want to check out which ones are most popular, you can use Google Trends (www.google.com/trends).

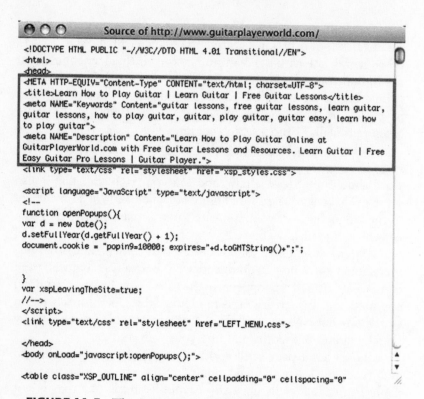

FIGURE 11.5 The Appearance of HTML Source Code Displaying a
Title and Meta Tags

Google also has a great tool to give you keyword ideas, along
with how many times each particular keyword is searched in a
month:

www.adwords.google.com/select/KeywordToolExternal.

One criteria that search engines use to rank a web site, besides
keywords and meta tags, is counting the number of links leading to
your web site. The more links you have coming to your web site,
the higher your site will rank. Additionally, the more popular a web
site is that links to your own, the higher the rating the search engine
will give your site. So a link from CNN.com or Microsoft.com will
hold more weight than a similar link from Joe's Barber Shop's
web page.

To increase the number of links pointing to your web site, you can team up with related web sites and swap links. If you ran a boating web site, you might link to a fishing equipment web site in return for them linking to your web site.

A great resource to hire a marketer who can help you rank higher in the search engines can be found through www.odesk.com. Just like any outsourcing project, which we'll talk more about in the outsourcing chapter, be sure to check references and see examples of their work.

Warning: There are a number of scam web sites and companies that will guarantee you top 10 placements for 10, 20, or more keywords for a hefty price tag of a few thousand dollars. They fill you with pipe dreams of generating massive traffic to your web site. But here's the catch: They rank you in the top 10 for keywords that almost nobody uses, therefore few, if any, other sites compete for those keywords. So your web site will be ranked at the top of Google for those keywords, but if nobody is searching for them, it does you no good. Please do not fall for this scam.

Signature Files

One free way to promote your web site is to place a blurb describing your site along with its address in your e-mail signature files. Now any e-mail message you send to others will contain your free advertisement. If others forward your message to their friends, your free advertisement spreads even further.

Since you're sending e-mail messages out all the time, you'd be foolish to pass up this chance to promote yourself at no cost. Many people even forward particularly interesting messages to their friends, so there's a good chance that some of your messages will eventually reach more people than you might ever meet yourself.

Make your signature files catchy, with a call to action that gives people a reason to visit your web site. For example, you might do something like this:

> "I lost 40 pounds with a new nutritional supplement. Find out how at www.abc.com."

or

> "P.S. I'm making money through 3 little known secrets of marketing, which you can get at www.abc.com."

If you are active in any online forums, include your signature with a link back to your web site any time you submit a post. Another benefit of leaving your web site link on a forum is that the search engines will count that as an incoming link to your web site and thus rank your site a bit higher.

Article Marketing

There's a crying need for content on the Internet, so you could be the one to fill that need through article writing. The basic idea is that you write a short article that provides useful information about a topic that you're knowledgeable about. At the end of the article, include your biography, along with a link to your web site, and submit the whole thing to various article web sites such as:

- Ezine Articles (http://ezinearticles.com)
- Article City (www.articlecity.com)
- Article Directory (www.articledirectory.com)
- GoArticles (www.goarticles.com)

Many of these articles wind up on other people's web sites that need fresh content to display. Not surprisingly, other businesses that put out newsletters also browse through these article sites looking for content they can use. Each time somebody uses your article, your web site address and author biography will appear, which means more links directing others back to you.

You will not get a ton of traffic from one article so the more you write the better. This is yet another great way to get links back to your web site for SEO. If you're not particularly excited about writing lots of articles, I highly recommend outsourcing the writing of your articles to a ghost writer. You should expect to pay $10 to $20 for a 400-word article typically written by someone overseas. You'll want to ensure that any article you pay for is original content. When you get an article back from your ghost writer, search a few of the sentences in Google to see if the article appears anywhere else online. If it does, you'll want to fire your ghost writer immediately.

Following are some outsourcing resources to find ghost writers:

- Elance (www.elance.com)
- Guru.com (www.guru.com)
- Agents of Value (www.agentsofvalue.com)

E-mail Newsletters

One way to stay in touch with customers and potential customers is through a free newsletter, which you can send out by e-mail. These newsletters typically provide useful information so people will want to read them, while also providing a medium for promoting your products and web site, as well as other web sites you are affiliated with.

Like e-mail messages, newsletters often get passed to others if they contain useful information, which means your newsletter could eventually wind up in the hands of other people who you may never have met or contacted before.

Here are a few tips for writing a good newsletter:

- *Be yourself:* Don't be afraid to express your personality. You want to build a relationship with your readers. Selling 101—people buy from people they know, like, and trust.
- *Be different:* The worst thing you can do is be boring. Find ways to be unique and stand out compared to the competition

in your market. People's lives, for the most part, are boring and any time you can liven up their day, you become a more appealing business partner.

- *Play off current events:* Figure out ways to link your product or service to what's happening in the world. If you sell a financial product, link it to overcoming our disastrous economy. If you're selling weight loss, link a story to a celebrity who lost a ton of weight. If you sell information on how to make money, call it the "John Doe Stimulus Plan," piggybacking President Barack Obama's stimulus plan, or call it the "Recession-Proof Your Income" newsletter. Be creative and even if there is not a direct tie-in, figure out a way to indirectly link a current story to your product or service.

- *Provide Value:* Don't be afraid to give away a tremendous amount of value in your newsletter. Many marketers are afraid that if they give away too many valuable tips in their newsletter, people will not buy their product. The opposite is true. What goes through your prospect's mind is that if you're giving away this much value for something free, the product you charge for must be *really* good.

- *Sell!:* It's great to provide valuable content, but if that's all you're doing you'll go broke. Almost always end your newsletter with a call to action to buy your product or an affiliate product based on your recommendation.

Search Engine Pay-Per-Click Advertising

One of the most common ways to advertise on the Internet is through sponsored search links—Google is the most popular. The way this works is that you bid on key words that define the maximum price you're willing to pay. When someone searches for a product or service that matches the keywords you've defined, your ad appears at the top or side of the search engine page. These are called "Sponsored Links."

Since people are already looking for your type of product, they usually don't see your ad as a nuisance but as an aid to help them get what they want. When they click on your ad, you get charged whether they buy something from you or not.

Buying keywords means that your ad can also appear in more than just search engine pages. Web site publishers all over the world use services such as Google AdSense to display ads within their own web pages. If your ads match the content of a web site's focus, your ads can literally appear in thousands of web sites that you may never know even exist.

As an advertiser, you must pay each time someone clicks on your ad. However, you can even specify a maximum dollar amount you want to pay within a fixed interval of time (such as one month). That way you won't risk overspending on your advertising budget.

The two biggest sites for advertising your web site through Internet ads are:

- Google Adwords (http://adwords.google.com)
- Yahoo Search Marketing (http://searchmarketing.yahoo.com)

Here's the key in creating successful text ads. Be creative and, once again, *stand out!* One of the most effective strategies for successful advertising, whether it be print or online, is to lead people to believe that buying your competitor's product will cause disappointment or loss. It's what I call a "warning" ad, which has been one of the most effective advertising methods used for decades. Here's how you might use a warning ad for someone who types in "weight loss."

The TRUTH about **Weight Loss**
WARNING! Read this BEFORE
you buy any **weight loss** product!

Weight Loss Secrets
Don't buy ANY **Weight Loss**
products until you read THIS ...

You can substitute just about any product in these examples to make your ad work.

Another quick recommendation on text ads is to put the keyword in the headline and body of the ad. You'll notice that in your search results, the keyword you searched is highlighted in the ad, which causes your ad to stand out. It's been proven that having the keyword in the ad increases the click-through rate (CTR), which is important because the better your click-through rate, the higher your ad will appear.

One of the best, and *free*, ways to generate keywords is by using a tool Google offers for free at www.google.com/sktool.

Ezine Advertising

The best advertising is targeted to the type of people most likely to buy your product or service and one of the best ways to target your ads to a particular group is through ezine advertising. That's why many web sites offer weekly ezines, which basically contain short articles loaded with useful tips related to a specific topic such as gardening, digital photography, or caring for your pet. These web sites send out regular ezines to keep in touch with their customers, but by purchasing ad space in these ezines, you can reach those same people, too.

Buying ads in an ezine is a win-win for everybody. Your ad reaches the exact group of people most inclined to buy your products or services, the ezine publisher gets payment from you to defray the cost of putting together and sending out ezines, and the ezine subscribers get exposed to your business, which offers them products that might be suited to their interests.

Unlike advertising in traditional print magazines or newspapers, ezine advertising is inexpensive and focused, giving you better results at far less cost. In comparison, ordinary magazine or newspaper advertising simply tries to reach as many people as possible, whether they have any interest in your business or not.

Even better, ezines are easy for people to copy and forward to their friends, which means a single ad in the right ezine can reach a large group of potential customers. Every ezine ad you place links directly back to your own web site, which can generate new traffic from multiple sources, boosting sales and driving up your ranking in the popular search engines at the same time.

To find an ezine, you can visit the top web sites in your same industry, or visit one of the following sites, which offers directories of ezines organized by topics. Browse through these lists of ezines and you can pinpoint the ones you think will best reach your potential customers:

- EzineAdvertising.com (www.EzineAdvertising.com)
- EzineAd.net (www.ezinead.net)
- Directory of Ezines (www.DirectorofEzines.com)

Face-to-Face Networking

When promoting your web site, don't overlook ordinary word of mouth advertising. Print business cards with your web site's address on them and pass these cards out to everyone you meet. Leave them in restaurants whenever you leave a tip, stuff them in envelopes every time you need to pay a bill, and hand them out as a way of introducing yourself in social and business settings. Advertising is a numbers game, so the more people see your web site address, the more people will take the time to visit your web site.

Recruiting Affiliates to Market Your Web Site

This has been, by far, the most powerful way I've been able to market my web sites online. My entire focus has been dedicated primarily to recruiting top affiliates.

A great way to gather successful affiliates is through affiliate networks, which I explained earlier in the chapter. And while I've had success through these networks, my success in finding huge affiliates has come much more so by creating a specific and targeted campaign to recruit them. Because there is such an art and science to this process, I've dedicated an entire chapter to the subject—you'll learn more in Chapter 15.

Selling Digital Products

Selling physical products over the Internet is popular, but there's always the hassle of shipping products and dealing with shipping delays, damaged products, and returns. Perhaps the most cost-effective way to make money on the Internet is by selling digital products, such as ebooks, audio/mp3 courses, or online video-based courses. Each of these cost virtually nothing to store and you can deliver them to your clients at no cost. Create it once, sell it multiple times, and you can create a business where your web site accepts orders and sends out the ebook automatically, so you don't have to do a thing.

If you're good at writing and have specialized knowledge in a particular subject you can create your own ebook. You can also find and repackage public domain content as your own information products. All works published in the United States before 1923 are in the public domain. In addition, anything published between 1923 and 1963 falls into the public domain if the author didn't renew the copyright.

Here are a couple of great resources for finding works in the public domain:

- Project Gutenberg (www.gutenberg.org): The first and largest single collection of free eBooks.
- LibriVox (www.LibriVox.org): Large collection of free audiobooks.

Another simple way to create a digital product is to buy one that includes the master reseller rights. This essentially means that you have the right to buy the product once, modify it, and sell it as many times without ever paying an additional fee or royalty. There are a ton of various web sites that will sell you the rights to digital products at incredibly affordable prices.

To find these, simply go to Google and type in "Resell Rights" or "Master Resale Rights" and you'll have plenty to choose from. Personally, I've never sold these products as my main product, but I have used them for bonuses to add value to my main product offering.

To create an ebook, all you need to do is create useful information in a word processor and save it as a PDF (Portable Document Format) file. If you don't want to write, use an audio recorder, capture your information through your spoken voice, and have your audio file transcribed into text. Some audio transcription services include:

- Transcriptions Service (www.transcriptionsservice.com)
- CastingWords (http://castingwords.com/store)
- Amazon Mechanical Turk (www.mturk.com/mturk/welcome)

Of course, you don't have to even transcribe your audio files into text at all since you could also sell your information as mp3 audio files. If you want to get even fancier, you can capture video of yourself and sell video files instead of, or in addition to, an ebook.

One way to make digital products even more appealing to potential customers is to use virtual cover software to create an image to display on your web site that makes your ebook look more professional. Likewise, if you're selling an audio or video course, you want to show a picture of a CD/DVD case. Showing a picture helps give a digital product a more tangible feel.

The problem is that your ebook, audio, or video course probably isn't packaged nicely so you can take a picture of it. That's where virtual cover programs come to the rescue.

These programs basically let you take any graphic design and morph that graphic design into different product images. If you had a picture, you could make that picture appear on a hard- or softcover book or on a CD/DVD case.

Here are a few resources to have your cover designed:

- Max Covers (www.maxcovers.com): I've used Max several times and he's always been on time and very affordable.
- Box Shot 3D (www.boxshot3d.com).
- Virtual Cover Creator (www.virtual-cover-creator.net).

Digital products offer the ultimate in sales convenience. Set up your web site to take orders and the moment a customer's credit card is approved, your web site can automatically e-mail the customer with the desired product for instant gratification with no intervention from you at all.

Web sites that sell digital products are like vending machines that dispense an unlimited number of products while being available to customers 24 hours a day, seven days a week. All you have to do is set up your marketing and cash the checks, making digital products one of the best choices for living the life of an Unemployed Millionaire.

The Real Money Is in the List

Selling any type of products online can certainly earn you plenty of income. However, the real fortune lies in collecting a database of e-mail addresses from customers and potential customers interested in your particular niche.

There are two main factors of critical importance to turning your e-mail list into profits:

- *Your e-mail list is targeted:* The phone directory is technically a list, but it's useless since none of the names are connected in any way. On the other hand, a list of 100 e-mail addresses of people interested in baseball is far more valuable because you can now send marketing messages to those people, selling products that appeal to their interests, such as baseball memorabilia or baseball documentaries. A huge mistake many new marketers make is e-mailing offers to people on their list with products that are not targeted to the interests of those in the database. If you've developed a list of people interested in gardening and you e-mail them an offer to buy baseball products, not only will they not buy, they'll remove themselves from your e-mail list.

- *You have created a relationship with your e-mail list:* Many e-mail marketing firms sell huge lists containing millions of e-mail addresses. While these lists may be targeted toward specific niches, they will rarely if ever produce a profit because the people on the list have no idea who you are. The key in list building is *quality*, not *quantity*. I'd take a list of 10,000 e-mail addresses who know me above 1,000,000 who have no idea who I am.

Building a Relationship with Your List Is Just Like Dating

Communicating regularly to your list is of vital importance. Many marketers make the mistake of e-mailing their list too infrequently because they're afraid of sending too many e-mails for fear that their members will unsubscribe. This may be counterintuitive, but the exact opposite is true. If you e-mail your database only once per month, they are actually *more* likely to unsubscribe because they tend to forget who you are in between e-mails.

Think of it like dating. If you date someone only once per month, the chances of building a long-term, stable relationship are pretty slim. And like dating, you also probably don't want to ask them out on a date every single day. Two to three times per week is what I've found to be the best frequency for effectively building a strong relationship with your list.

How to Start Building Your List

The best way to capture an e-mail address is to offer free information, such as an ebook, report, mp3, or newsletter. To get this free gift, visitors must give you their e-mail address. This is what is commonly referred to as a lead capture page or a "squeeze" page. Immediately after your prospect fills out the squeeze page, he or she should be presented with a sales letter marketing your product.

If you'd like to see some examples of ultra-successful squeeze pages, check out these links:

- www.Nitro-Traffic.com: Gives away 10 traffic secrets.
- www.DoubleYourDating.com/channels/articles: One of the most successful, and widely plagiarized headlines, online.
- www.VideoGeneratorSoftware.com: Great use of video.

The absolute best source I've found to create squeeze pages, with no technical knowledge necessary, can be found at www.MarketingGenerator.net.

Whether you're selling your own products, or you're selling products from other people as an affiliate, creating your own squeeze page is a great idea for several reasons.

The first reason may run contrary to what the average person would naturally think, which is that surely a lot fewer people will fill out their personal information, so fewer people will see your sales page. And while this is 100 percent true, what you must realize is that, on average, a person should be followed up with five times in order to make a buying decision. If you send people directly to a sales page, you have no opportunity to follow up with them. But when you've collected their e-mail address on a squeeze page, you can send them an unlimited number of follow-up e-mails until they either buy your product or unsubscribe from your list. So while you'll get fewer people to look at your sales letter, in most cases you'll get more people who actually buy.

The other reason why it's great to use a squeeze page is that you have the opportunity to sell potential buyers multiple products by e-mail. If you just lead them to a sales page, the only product you have the opportunity to sell them is the product on that page. But if you sell dog grooming products, and your sales page is for a dog grooming brush, once you have their e-mail you can now market a whole range of dog grooming products to them even if they don't buy your brush. You can market to them any number of similar products that can either be yours or those of another web site where you earn an affiliate commission.

E-mail Service Providers

To take advantage of using a squeeze page, or any other method to collect an e-mail address, you'll need an e-mail service to send the e-mails. Such e-mail services let you automate your advertising campaigns. For example, the first time someone gives you his or her name and e-mail address, you might want the person to receive a welcoming e-mail message right away along with his or her free gift.

A day or two later, you might want to follow up with another message, offering useful information along with a promotion for one of your products or services. As long as someone allows you to send him or her e-mail, your e-mail service can send an endless stream of marketing messages to your list of motivated prospects. At any given time, only a small percentage of these prospects will buy from you, but since your entire e-mail marketing campaign is automated, it happens while you sleep.

Your e-mail service sends out messages, your prospects buy from you, and you get to cash the checks. It's the perfect business model for an Unemployed Millionaire.

There are a number of e-mailing services, from $20 a month to $2,000 a month or more, depending on your list size. If you're just starting out with a small list, I'd recommend Aweber above all others. I've met the owner and many of the company's employees, and it is the most trusted company I've seen in the direct marketing world for small business owners. I'll provide a list of a few others that are also highly reputable. They have almost all of the same features and benefits so it really all comes down to your personal preference and who you feel most comfortable with.

For smaller businesses:

- Aweber (www.Aweber.com)
- Get Response (www.GetResponse.com)
- iContact (www.iContact.com)

For larger businesses:

- Silverpop (www.Silverpop.com) After analyzing the higher-end solutions, I chose Silverpop for my company. Excellent functionality and tremendous service.
- Lyris (www.lyris.com)
- Exact Target (www.ExactTarget.com)

With so many different ways to make money and market your business over the Internet, you have no reason not to take advantage of these opportunities today. Internet marketing is a rapidly growing field that provides tremendous opportunities to make money from advertising revenue, selling other people's products, or selling your own products. Best of all, you can start an Internet business anywhere in the world (as long as you have an Internet connection) and make money automatically; this makes Internet marketing one of the potentially most profitable ways to become an Unemployed Millionaire.

Real Estate Investing

The best investment on earth is earth.

—Louis Glickman

The best business is one where as many people as possible can be your customers, and nothing is more universal than real estate. Put simply, everyone needs to live somewhere. With real estate, you can either sell or rent property to others. When you sell property, you can often make more in a single transaction than you might normally make in an entire month or even an entire year of working in a job. If you rent property, you can earn a monthly income that can supplement or eventually even exceed your current income.

What makes real estate investing so attractive for Unemployed Millionaires is that you can buy and sell real estate anywhere in the world, although it's usually best to start right in your own neighborhood. No matter where you live, you know more about that part of town than any outside investor could possibly know. Every day, you know which areas are growing, which areas are declining, which areas are the most popular, and which areas are the most dangerous. In short, you already know which areas are potentially the most lucrative with no real estate training whatsoever other than just living in the area.

Here's another great reason to be involved in real estate. Over the long-term, real estate prices always go up. While prices may drop in the short-term, real estate gradually appreciates in value over the long-term. Ask any number of senior citizens how much money they could have made if they had bought a house in a certain area a long time ago. Chances are good they will tell you how little they could have bought a house a while ago and how much that house would be worth today.

Perhaps the true value of real estate lies in the fact that banks will loan you money to buy real estate, but few banks will loan the same amount of money for you to start any other type of business. Ask a bank for $200,000 to buy a house and if you have decent credit, you can likely get a loan. Ask that same bank for $200,000 to invest in the bank's own stock on the stock market, and the bank won't even consider loaning you any money.

Perhaps the most important feature of real estate is leverage, which essentially lets you buy on credit. When you go to a store and want a new pair of shoes, you can either pay in full with cash, or you can pay on credit. The same principle applies to real estate.

If you have $10,000, you can use that money as a partial down payment to buy a much more valuable piece of property, such as a $100,000 condo. By putting down 10 percent, you now control property worth far more than the amount of money you invested. If you were to invest $10,000 in any other traditional investment and received a 10 percent return, you would earn $1,000 on your $10,000 investment.

However, if you buy a $100,000 condo with that same $10,000, and the $100,000 home appreciates by 10 percent, that home is now worth $110,000, giving you a net profit of $10,000. Your initial $10,000 investment has returned a $10,000 profit for a 100 percent return.

Despite economic conditions, real estate has always been one of the safest forms of wealth-building available. You don't need any special training to buy and sell real estate, nor do you necessarily need a large amount of money to get started. Real estate investing, like all forms of wealth-building, does require effort and time. You may not get rich overnight, but through consistent effort over time, anyone can use real estate to build their net worth from nothing to six or seven figures.

Real Estate Investing Principle Number 1

There are numerous ways to make money in real estate, but the *key principle* I've found from my success, and the successful real estate investors I work with, is to be in a position to make a profit right away without betting on appreciation.

Many new real estate investors buy a house at market price with the assumption that the house will appreciate quickly, thereby earning them their profits. If you are investing purely for the long term, that may be okay, but there is no guarantee that any area will appreciate over the next 5 to 10 years, no matter how much it's appreciated over the last 5 to 10 years.

A perfect example for this is the real estate market in Las Vegas. For the past several years, Vegas real estate has been booming and growing at double digits each year. Investors flooded the market picking up any property they could, thinking they could do no wrong because of the skyrocketing home prices. That strategy worked for a few years until the market completely crashed, leaving investors with homes they are completely upside down on. (They owe much more than they could sell the house for.)

Because market prices and economic fluctuations can be so unpredictable, the only surefire strategy for real estate investing is to pick up property at below retail prices.

How to Buy Real Estate at Wholesale Prices

Like any business, the key is to buy low and sell high. The difference between the price you paid and the selling price is the profit, whether you're selling a can of soup or a three-bedroom home on a half-acre of land.

The Power of Asking

The simplest way to buy real estate at a low price is simply to ask. Just because someone lists a home at $145,000 doesn't mean he or she won't accept something less. Perhaps the seller needs to move in three weeks and he or she just wants to get rid of the house as quickly as possible. Maybe the seller just listed the home at a higher price in hopes of getting it, but realistically expects something much less. If the property has been on the market for several months, the seller may just want to get rid of the home because he or she is tired of waiting for a better price. In real estate, you never know the seller's motivation.

If you offer to pay a lower price, many buyers will refuse. It doesn't cost you anything to ask for a lower price and if the seller won't negotiate, then you walk away and look for another home. As a real estate investor, you don't need a particular home; you just need a home that you can buy at a wholesale price.

It may take several weeks or even several months to find a bargain home, so you may spend long amounts of time with no immediate profit. But all you need is one great deal and you're immediately ahead of the game.

To speed up the process, the more offers you make, the greater your chance of success. A very successful friend of mine uses what I would call an almost mass-marketing approach. He'll do a little research on multiple properties and simply submit lowball offers where he can't go wrong. Because he's making so many offers, he picks up incredible deals that most investors would never get because they're afraid of offending the seller. Remember, it never hurts to ask.

Besides asking for a lower price, another popular way to buy real estate at wholesale prices is through probate. When people die, they often leave behind property they lived in or owned. In many cases, the inheritors don't live near that property and probably have never seen it. When multiple people inherit a property, they can't divide a house into several pieces, so the first thing they want to do is sell it, usually as quickly as possible.

Many real estate investors simply visit the local county courthouse to find a list of probate properties. Then they contact the inheritors about the property. Of course, not everyone who inherits property will want to sell it cheaply, but such property owners are more motivated to sell quickly than the typical homeowner, which makes probate properties an excellent source of wholesale homes.

How to Get an Upgraded Hotel Suite 75 Percent of the Time

When I stay in hotels, those I'm traveling with are always amazed at how I consistently get upgraded rooms almost every time. Want to know the secret? It's simple really; I just ask!

When I'm checking into a hotel, I always approach the counter with a big smile on my face and ask the person behind the desk how he or she is doing. It's amazing how few people take the time to ask about them. The vast majority of guests that check in are self-absorbed and can barely mutter like a robot, "John Doe checking in," without even as much as a simple hello. Also, I almost always pay the person behind the desk a sincere compliment (he or she has a great smile, tie, jewelry, etc.,) or I do my best to say something funny. I'll look at the person's name tag and say something silly like "John! I came all the way from Dallas to meet you—they said you were going to take good care of me, is that right?" Or I might say "Mary, where have you been all my life!?" just to be silly.

Now I'm definitely no comedian, but the simple fact that I'm being playful with the person is so out of the ordinary that he or she will typically laugh and show a big smile. You see, by making that person smile, I'm adding value to their day. And when you give something out, it's typically a lot easier to get something in return. So after I've built some rapport with him or her, I give my name and as the person is pulling me up on the computer I simply ask, "Is there any chance I can get a complimentary upgrade tonight?"

Almost every time, if there is space available, I get the upgrade.

Use the Recession to Your Advantage

Due to the economic crisis we're in right now, many real estate investors will amass fortunes over the next few years through foreclosures. When homeowners can't afford to make their mortgage payments, they receive a notice of default from their bank. These homeowners are now highly motivated to sell their homes to repay the bank before foreclosure, which can damage their credit for years.

Visit a web site like www.CurrentForeclosures.com to see the number of foreclosures in every state. By tracking this information, you see which states have the highest number of foreclosures (and thus the greatest number of investment opportunities).

One simple way to find foreclosures, or any type of real estate for that matter, is just to drive around looking for "For Sale" signs. Often a house will go on the market before the agent has time to list it on the Multiple Listing Service (MLS) where other agents can spot it. If you find a house with a new For Sale sign in the front yard, you can often swoop in and grab it before anyone else is even aware it's available. Be especially alert for any For Sale signs that mention "Bank-owned," "Foreclosure," or "Bank repo," since this identifies the home as a foreclosed property.

Another way to find foreclosed properties is to visit a major bank's web site, such as one of the following:

- Bank of America (http://bankofamerica.reo.com/search)
- Countrywide (www.countrywide.com/purchase/f_reo.asp)
- Chase Mortgage (http://mortgage.chase.com/pages/other/ co_properties_landing.jsp)

Although you can find bank-owned properties through these web sites, you still have to contact the real estate agent assigned to these properties.

Many banks get rid of their foreclosed properties through home auctions. Generally an auction causes people to bid higher due to the frenzy of auction, but you can still pick up bargains if you're patient. Some of the more popular real estate auction houses include:

- Bid 4 Assets (http://www.bid4assets.com)
- Real Estate Disposition Corporation (www.ushomeauction .com)
- United Country Auction Services (www.ucauctionservices .com)
- Williams & Williams (www.williamsauction.com)

Two popular Internet foreclosure web sites include Foreclosures.com (www.foreclosures.com) and Realty Trac (www.realtytrac.com).

Another simple way to find foreclosed properties is to visit your local county courthouse to find the addresses of homes that have received a notice of default. You can then contact these home-owners directly. By offering to buy their homes, you can rescue them from an unfortunate situation while buying the home at an attractive price.

If a home goes into foreclosure, the bank winds up owning the property. Unfortunately, banks don't make money by owning property, so they'll try to sell these homes off as quickly as possible. Since the bank has already written the home off as a loss, they'll often list the home at a low price just to get rid of it.

Banks aren't the only ones who wind up owning property they don't want. The government often seizes property through tax liens (when people fail to pay taxes) or by seizing criminal assets. Like banks, government agencies don't want to own homes so they sell them at a low price to get rid of them.

Ultimately, the lower the price you can pay for real estate, the better your chances of making a profit. Finding low-priced real estate takes work, but the results are almost always worth it.

Flipping and Renting Real Estate

The simplest and most obvious way to make money in real estate is known as "flipping." That's when you buy property and sell it to someone else at a higher price. In a growing market flipping is a simple and lucrative strategy. In a slow real estate market, flipping is difficult, but not impossible.

To improve your chances of selling a home at a higher price, make simple improvements that make a home more attractive without spending a lot of money. Sometimes just painting the outside or inside makes a tired old house look brand new. Mow the grass and do simple landscaping to give the house curb appeal to attract potential buyers.

Most people want to buy a home to live in, so they want a home that's move-in ready. Buying slightly run-down homes and spending a little time fixing them up makes a dumpy home suddenly look far more appealing, thus allowing you to sell it for a higher price.

A second way to make money in real estate is through renting. Check the average rent in an area. If you buy a home at a price where your monthly mortgage payment (including taxes and insurance) is less than the monthly rent you can collect, this generates positive cash flow right away because your renters pay your mortgage. As your mortgage goes down over time, your rents gradually go up to earn greater profits.

Flipping and renting are the two most common ways to make money in real estate, but a combination works as well. For example, you might buy a home but find that you can't flip it easily. Put renters in and have them pay your mortgage while you wait until the real estate market improves.

Rent to Own with Lease Options

Another technique is known as a lease option. Basically this combines renting and selling. If you've ever seen places that offer lease-to-own furniture, you already understand this principle. With a lease option, you put renters in a home while offering them the option of paying an additional fee (such as an extra $200 to $1,000 a month) as a down payment toward eventually purchasing the house after a fixed period of time (such as one or two years).

At the end of this time period, the renters have a choice. They can apply part of their rental payments toward the previously agreed upon price for the home, or they can choose not to buy the house and leave. If the renters choose to buy, you have a guaranteed sale and profit. If they choose to leave, you keep their additional down payments.

With the banks tightening their lending qualifications during this economic crisis, finding people willing to accept a lease option is easier than ever. Many people would love to own a home, but simply cannot due to poor credit or lack of credit. In many cases you can charge retail prices or even slightly higher for homes with lease options. If it weren't for the availability of a lease option, many would have no way to buy a home otherwise.

However, if you're offering a lease option to someone with poor credit, make sure you charge a down payment (which would be a security deposit for a rental) equivalent to two to four times what it would cost to simply rent a home. If you don't require the person to have any skin in the game, he or she will be a lot more likely to default on monthly payments, just like normal rental property. Trust me, I know from personal experience.

No Money Down Techniques

Perhaps the most amazing secret in real estate is that you can even make money with no money down. This simply means none of your money is at risk; you're actually using other people's money to buy real estate.

At the simplest level, find bargain-priced homes for other people, typically investors. Most people don't know how to find homes at wholesale prices and many investors don't want to take the time to search for these properties. You can match these low-priced homes with people looking for a bargain and take a finder's fee for your efforts. This is commonly known as bird-dogging.

This lets you make money in real estate without ever spending a single dime of your own money. All you have to do is find a list of people who want to buy a house, find out what type of house they want, and then go find homes matching their criteria. You'll find plenty of investors by visiting local real estate investment groups.

Be sure to sign a contract with potential buyers and investors that specifies that they'll pay you a finder's fee if you find a home that they'll buy, and when you find a home that matches an individual buyer's criteria, you will direct him or her to the seller to close the deal.

Spending time to earn finder's fees may not fit the profile of an Unemployed Millionaire since you have to keep looking for low-priced homes and finding new buyers. However, this method is how many real estate investors get started because it requires putting none of their own money at risk. Once they gain enough experience and earn enough money from finder's fees, they can buy low-priced homes themselves for flipping or renting.

Another no money down technique is to partner with somebody who does have money. You find the low-priced homes, your partner buys them, and you split the profits when you flip (sell) or rent the property. By not risking any of your own money, you can get started in real estate and make money right away.

Ultimately, the key is to start by only buying properties when you can buy them at wholesale prices. Once you buy a house at below market value, you'll have multiple options for profit.

Getting Started in Real Estate

Generally the first step to getting started in real estate is finding a real estate agent, although this isn't always necessary. If you're simply finding low-priced homes for other people to collect a finder's fee, you won't need a real estate agent at all. Even if you're buying and selling homes, you can avoid using a real estate agent and just hire a real estate attorney.

However, for most people, a real estate agent can be a valuable ally. Agents have the experience in what type of houses to look for and what problems might occur that the average person may never know about. Real estate agents can also help sift through the MLS, which is a computer database listing nearly every house on the market. Your agent can help you find bargain properties through the MLS much faster than you might be able to do yourself. A good real estate agent can also tell you which areas of town are popular with buyers and renters, and which areas aren't.

Second, start looking at the different areas where you live to get a feel for typical home prices and monthly rents. Look for areas to avoid (high crime rate) and look for areas that are growing due to their proximity to mass transit, desirable neighborhoods, or high growth areas. Many cities and local police departments have web sites that provide crime statistics for their community. While it's tempting to look at multimillion dollar homes and dream about buying and selling these types of properties, there are far fewer buyers and sellers in that price range.

The most profitable properties to buy, sell, and rent are generally three-bedroom, two-bath houses (abbreviated as 3BR/2BA) or two-bedroom, one-bath condominiums (2BR/1BA). Statistically speaking, homes and condos that meet these criteria are the easiest to sell and rent. Homes with more than three bedrooms can be more difficult to sell since people may not want the extra space, and homes with only one or two bedrooms are hard to sell and rent because most people want an extra guest room or office.

Third, don't be intimidated by all the legalities involved in buying and selling real estate. Basically, every deal boils down to negotiating a price that's acceptable to both the buyer and seller. If you ever need help, you can turn to your real estate agent or a real estate attorney for guidance.

Don't be afraid to switch real estate agents if necessary. If you don't feel that an agent is answering your questions or helping you as much as you would like, feel free to look for another one. There are plenty of agents available so take your time interviewing them until you find one you like.

Fourth, speed up your progress in real estate investing by looking for a mentor who can teach you shortcuts and spare you a lot of wasted effort and costly financial mistakes. A mentor should be someone who is currently investing and making money in real estate. Do what you can to learn from such mentors because their knowledge will shave years off your learning curve.

Fifth, treat real estate investing like a business and let everyone around you know that you buy and sell real estate. You never know when a chance conversation with a waitress or stranger can lead you to a bargain property that nobody else knows about.

Sixth, remember that like any business, real estate investing may not give you quick riches overnight. In fact, you may need to spend several months looking for a bargain before you find a property that meets your criteria. Even if you just buy one house a year, you'll own ten homes after ten years. Imagine how much monthly rent you can receive from ten properties, especially when each home mortgage keeps dropping over time while the rent keeps increasing over time.

In general, the two-step process for investing in real estate involves:

- Finding bargain-priced homes.
- Flipping (selling) or renting (with the option of selling it at a later date).

Find a home at a low price and you can sell it for a quick profit, or rent it out so your renters pay your mortgage while giving you extra cash every month as well. Remember, everyone needs to live somewhere and every property offers its own unique advantages. By using the principles of leverage to buy property with little or no money down, real estate offers an excellent opportunity for anyone, regardless of age or educational background, to become an Unemployed Millionaire.

Part III

Managing and Growing Your Business

13

The Stress-Free Outsourcing and Management System

"Management" means, in the last analysis, the substitution of thought for brawn and muscle, of knowledge for folkways and superstition, and of cooperation for force. It means the substitution of responsibility for obedience to rank, and of authority of performance for the authority of rank.

—Peter F. Drucker

If I offered to give you a million dollars, would you take it? Most people would probably say yes. Now what if I offered you a million dollars, but only if you were willing to stay with the money inside a bank vault and never come out? Now would you take the money?

I'm sure you would say no, which proves my point. Nobody really wants more money. What everyone wants are the benefits of money, whether it's the ability to buy anything you want, pursue your dreams, take vacations to exotic locations, or just have time to watch your children grow up. Money isn't the goal—it's a vehicle for getting to your goal.

The last thing you want is for your business to control you rather than you controlling your businesses. You don't want to create another job for yourself where you're locked into an office eight hours (or more) a day, doing things you don't really want to do.

That's why I've embraced a stress-free management system to keep my business running smoothly and profitably while still allowing me the free time to choose when I want to work and for how long. What I'm going to teach you in this chapter is how to manage a highly profitable business *and* a highly enjoyable personal life without making sacrifices to either one.

To succeed in business over the long-term, you'll need to duplicate yourself by hiring employees or by outsourcing work to others. This lets you focus on the work that's most important to you (or just the most fun) while letting other people take care of the necessary details that you wouldn't have time to do yourself. By leveraging the time of other people, you can spend your time on anything that directly influences profits and puts more money into your pocket.

Whether you're hiring employees or outsourcing your work, you'll need a system to manage them. What I'm going to cover next is a very specific three-part management system that's worked wonders for me.

Managing a Staff

Hiring your own employees may be more expensive than outsourcing, but it can be especially useful for keeping a person's talents working just for you and performing jobs that require a person's physical presence. If you want to build a company generating tens of millions of dollars a year, you may outsource many tasks, but you'll most likely need to have a core team centrally located in an office.

When you hire employees, you have the added responsibility of managing them. Many business owners make the false assumption that in order to make employees more productive and retain them, you must raise their pay. But when you look at employee satisfaction surveys, you find that monetary compensation is almost never the number one motivation.

Several factors that consistently rate higher than pay are an enjoyable working environment and the culture of the company. I'm going to share with you one simple creative idea that was incredibly inexpensive but created a major shift in the productivity of our customer service department. I'm giving this example not because I think you should necessarily implement it, but rather to show you how thinking creatively can add to your bottom line.

It was a challenge for our customer service department to stay caught up with our customer support ticketing system and answer e-mails. We had just hired a new customer service representative and we still couldn't catch up. We were about to hire another employee when I had our customer service manager test a new system.

We implemented a program called "Free Movie Fridays." If the team is 100 percent caught up on support tickets and e-mails Monday through Thursday, they get to take a two-hour lunch in our conference room to watch a movie. The company pays for the movie rental and provides lunch, which is by far less expensive than hiring new employees.

What happens? The customer service team is motivated all week to stay caught up. They're also motivated to make sure their teammates are caught up since one employee lagging behind will cause them all to miss out on a free lunch, an extra hour off, and watching a movie.

Since implementing Free Movie Fridays, our customer service team has stayed caught up almost every single week for over a year now. The savings from not having to hire additional customer service reps has been significant, but the real, immeasurable value has been in the improved customer satisfaction.

The Simple Three-Step Management Formula

Have you ever wanted a simple, concise management system that facilitates effective communication, continual progress toward your company's objectives, and extreme accountability? If so, here's a formula that worked wonders for my company.

When we grew from zero to over $4 million per year in sales in less than two years, I suddenly had a management and productivity nightmare. Our small, committed staff blossomed to a team of approximately 15 people. That's when we started missing deadlines and not following through on promises made to each other.

My solution was to work harder and just take over projects that my staff members did not finish on time. This continued for almost a year until I finally got fed up enough to find another way.

I realized that I was working solely "in" the business rather than "on" the business. When I stepped back from this cycle of insanity and started analyzing the real reason we weren't progressing, I realized I had to get out of pure production mode and learn how to manage others. After interviewing a few team members, I realized that when I delegated a project, not only did I not communicate the project completely (assuming they could read my mind), I wouldn't ask them about it until the deadline had passed.

What I found out was that they were confused from the beginning on what exactly to do because I didn't explain the project thoroughly. We missed deadlines because I didn't hold them accountable in any manner and they were afraid to ask questions for fear of being labeled incompetent. One simple management formula I implemented created a major shift in the productivity of our organization. This management system can be broken into three parts. The first part is what I call "The Daily Four."

Step 1: The Daily Four

Each manager who reports directly to me is responsible for submitting a daily report that should take no more than five to ten minutes to prepare. In that e-mail he or she simply answers four questions:

1. What are your top three priorities?
   (Having the manager list their priorities every day keeps them focused on what's most important, and allows me to ensure,

based on question 2, if he or she is working toward the most important goals.)

2. What results did you produce today?
   (Note: I used to ask what the manager "did" that day. I'd get a laundry list of items that didn't contribute to any bottom line results. By using the word "results" he or she is focused on production rather than simply activity.)

3. Problems or challenges?

4. What questions do you have for me?

After less than two weeks, almost everyone was more satisfied because of the enhanced communication and the tremendous increase in productivity we began to see as a company.

Warning: Please learn from my mistakes on this. Any employee who continually refuses to send you daily reports needs to be immediately let go. Give a warning or two first, but when someone cannot commit to a five- to ten-minute daily e-mail, he or she is certainly not committed to the success of your company.

Step 2: The Master Project List

The second part of this system involves what I call our "Master Project List." It's basically a community spreadsheet created using Google Docs so everyone can access it through a computer. Each manager has a tab listing each project, the deadline, project percentage complete, and notes. That way each manager can log in to this project list, keep track of his or her own priorities, and see what every other manager is working on. This helps keep each manager's tasks clear while encouraging communication among managers since they can better understand what everyone in the company is doing.

There are quite a few very affordable web-based project management solutions that offer a much broader management system that I'm talking about here. We've attempted to use two or three over the years that actually worked great. But because they had so many features, required log-ins, and so forth, we always ended up abandoning them. Because we use Gmail's corporate e-mail solution, an ordinary Google Docs spreadsheet has been a much simpler option that we've been able to use consistently.

If you'd like to research a more robust web-based solution, here are a few fantastic resources:

- Base Camp (www.BaseCampHQ.com)
- Quick Base (www.QuickBase.com)
- Work Zone (www.WorkZone.com)

Using Google Docs

Most people already know how to use a word processor and maybe a spreadsheet. Unfortunately, when people create a file in a word processor or spreadsheet, that file stays on their computer's hard drive. If you share that file with someone else, now you have the headache of having two identical files. Suppose you change one file but someone else changes the second file? Which file contains the latest changes?

To avoid this hassle of tracking multiple files scattered between different computers, use Google Docs, which provides a word processor and spreadsheet that you can use directly through any browser connected to the Internet.

The main advantage of Google Docs is that you can save your files directly on Google's servers so you only have one copy of the file at all times. You can password protect that file so only certain people can view and modify that file, but if somebody does modify that file, everyone sees the changes instantly. In fact, you can even collaborate in real-time on a single document among multiple people, which is great for managing our outsourced remote employees.

Best of all, Google Docs is completely free, so there's no excuse not to investigate it and see how it might help your business run smoothly and more efficiently.

Step 3: Weekly Accountability Meetings

The third part of my management system involves weekly management meetings. Each manager goes quickly through each project, gives an update, and gets feedback for anything needed to complete it. Keeping everyone informed is a powerful communication tool, but above that is the power of group accountability.

No manager wants to miss deadlines in front of his or her peers. It becomes incredibly obvious when one manager is the weak link in the chain because he or she is consistently missing deadlines and not showing progress from one week to the other. This weekly meeting also creates team camaraderie and allows for open dialogue between different departments so they can all help each other.

After implementing this system, my company went from a $4 million a year company to an approximately $10 million per year company in less than two years. The key is simply to increase communication and enforce accountability so people focus on results and not just action.

Outsourcing

If you deprive yourself of outsourcing and your competitors do not, you're putting yourself out of business.

—Lee Kuan Yew

In the traditional brick and mortar business world, you had to hire a new person if you needed more help. If that person didn't work out, you'd have to fire and replace him or her. Outsourcing is far simpler because you don't hire a person and pay for healthcare, equipment, supplies, insurance, taxes, or additional benefits to attract quality employees. Instead, you hire a person's services on a contract basis, either ongoing or a onetime job.

For example, let's say you need to design and print signs, flyers, or menus. Rather than hire a desktop publisher and graphic artist as an employee (and buy the necessary graphic design software and printing equipment), you could just outsource this work to a graphic design artist who already has all the necessary equipment to design and print your material.

Outsourcing isn't just for onetime projects, such as writing a white paper or designing a web site; it can be used for work traditionally done by employees. If you need work done that doesn't require the person to be in the same office building, you can outsource the work to a virtual employee.

For example, most companies don't want to deal with the hassle of hiring accountants and bookkeepers to print payroll checks for their employees. Instead, they hire an outside payroll and bookkeeping service to do the work. Some other tasks suitable for outsourcing include:

Customer support

Writing articles, ad copy, white papers, and so forth

Computer tasks (such as programming, web page designing, or desktop publishing)

Manufacturing

Shipping and fulfillment

Hiring

Outsourcing gives you the freedom to literally change workers at any time. When you hire a traditional employee and that person doesn't do the job you wanted, you can either focus on training the employee (spending time and money) or firing and hiring a new employee (wasting time). With outsourcing, if you don't like the work of one person or company, you can choose another one for the same or even less cost.

Some popular sites to find people willing to perform different jobs include:

eLance (www.elance.com)

RentACoder (www.rentacoder.com)

Workaholics4Hire (www.workaholics4hire.com)

PHPCareer.com (www.phpcareer.com)

Brickwork India (www.BrickworkIndia.com)

Odesk (www.odesk.com)

Agents of Value (www.agentsofvalue.com)

To use these sites, you post a description of the work you need done and then people bid on your project. Many people bidding on projects will include their resume so you can see their work and experience. If they've been involved with a particular web site for a while, they may even have customer satisfaction ratings that can help you identify who might be more reliable.

While it's tempting to choose the lowest bidder, you also want to take into account the person's skill level, experience in working with projects similar to your own, feedback others have left about that person, and (most importantly) samples of their work. I've used these outsourcing companies countless times to handle everything from graphic design, copywriting, article writing, programming, and even developing instructional courses.

Many of the people I've hired have been from India, China, or the Philippines, where the average income is $200 to $500 a month or less. In many cases, you'll pay pennies on the dollar, which allows you the ability to hire as many as 10 outsourced employees for the cost of hiring one locally. It's also a huge blessing to the people you hire because you're paying them more than they could earn in their own country.

When you first post a description of your project on a site like eLance, it's a good idea to keep your project description fairly vague until you actually start choosing a specific person. Many people study these outsourcing sites, looking for ideas on projects that they can copy and use, too. If you post a project description for a new program that you want to develop, a competitor might see your project description and literally steal your idea.

After you've chosen a handful of potential workers, specify exactly what you need and expect so the other person knows what the entire project entails. What's especially important is that if you hire others to create something for you such as an ebook or computer program, make sure you reserve the rights to the product in your name. When working with outsiders, you're providing work-for-hire, which means after you pay for the work product, you never have to pay another penny to anyone again, whatever you do with your product.

Outsourcing can be useful for temporary work, but if you find someone particularly reliable, you might want to hire that person to work full time so you don't risk losing him or her to another company.

The Magic of Virtual Assistants

Basically a virtual assistant helps you do whatever tasks you need done, thus freeing up your limited time to focus on more productive projects that generate revenue. For example, you could keep track of your own schedule, or you could hire a personal assistant. Doing this job yourself wastes valuable time but hiring an assistant may be too expensive. That's where virtual assistants step in.

Virtual assistants do tasks for you, which typically require using a computer. A virtual assistant can do anything a personal assistant can do except for tasks that require a physical presence, such as picking up your dry cleaning or taking your car to get an oil change. Some tasks perfectly suited for a virtual assistant include:

Typing and data entry
Research for potential clients or partners
Organizing and responding to e-mail
Responding to phone calls
Making travel arrangements
Conducting market research and competitive analysis
Managing marketing campaigns
Following up with other employees on tasks you've delegated
General research
Writing articles, blogs, letters, and white papers
Order processing
Maintaining a web site
Graphic design
Transcription
Telephone support

Let's say you decide that a blog could be an effective marketing tool, yet you simply don't have the time to set one up and keep it up to date. Let your virtual assistant write and run it, with feedback from you.

Need to research your competition but don't quite understand all the different ways to analyze your competitors through the Internet? Hire a virtual assistant to do this work for you and just hand you the results.

Need to write a letter? Dictate your thoughts into a recorder, send the audio file to your virtual assistant, and have your virtual assistant transcribe your thoughts into print.

Practically anything you don't want to do with a computer, a virtual assistant can do for you instead. Initially, working with a virtual assistant may be a little awkward as you get used to delegating tasks and your virtual assistant learns your work habits and preferences. After a while, your virtual assistant will better understand what you want done and how you want it done. You'll find that it's like cloning yourself to do tasks you either don't want to do or even can't do. To find a virtual assistant, visit one of the following:

- Get Friday (https://getfriday.com)
- oDesk (www.odesk.com)
- Best Jobs Philippines (www.bestjobs.ph)
- Virtual Assistants For You (www.va4u.com)
- Global Sky (www.global-sky.com)
- Internet Girl Friday (www.internetgirlfriday.com)
- Virtual Assistants, Inc. (www.virtualassistant.org)
- AssistU (www.assistu.com)
- International Association of Virtual Assistants (www.ivaa.org)

By going through any of these web sites, you're sure to find plenty of potential virtual assistants who live all over the world, including the United States, India, Canada, China, or the Philippines. To find the best virtual assistant, or any other outsourced employee, interview him or her using GoToMeeting (www.gotomeeting. com), which is a service that lets you talk and share your computer screens with each other through an Internet connection.

Give each prospective virtual assistant a common task that you'll need done and watch him or her to make sure the assistant is computer savvy. For example, you might have the person write some simple code, create an Excel spreadsheet from data you give him or her, sort a list of names and addresses, or any number of tasks that proves the person can do what you need done.

To increase your chances of finding the perfect virtual assistant, hire two virtual assistants and compare their work. Then keep the one who does the best job or does it the quickest.

One point to keep in mind is the location of your virtual assistant. For example, if you need work done right away, you may prefer finding a virtual assistant who lives in your same time zone. That way your virtual assistant will be available during normal business hours. However, if you only need someone to do tasks that can be done at any time of the day, such as processing orders or designing a newsletter, then it might not matter if your virtual assistant lives in a time zone that's several hours ahead or behind your own.

Depending on the amount of work and the type of work you need done, this is what you can expect to pay for a virtual assistant:

- $180 to $800 per month if you hire the person directly ($1.13 to $5.00 per hour)
- $800 to $2,000 per month if you hire the person through a third party ($5.00 to$12.00 per hour)

Is It Worth It?

Obviously you have to consider what your own time is worth. Many people only need a virtual employee for short-term projects, such as designing a web site. Other times, you may need a virtual employee on a regular basis, such as sorting and responding to your e-mail every day.

Think of all those trivial, but necessary tasks that you need to do but would rather not, and imagine how much more free time you could have if you outsourced this work. If your time is worth

$50 an hour, paying a virtual assistant $10 an hour literally saves you money. Don't make the mistake of trying to do everything yourself. You'll find that the more you delegate and outsource to others, the more time you can focus on what you really love about your business. That will be healthy for both you and your pocketbook in the long run.

14

Outsource Your Marketing through Joint Venturing

Good marketers create sales. Great marketers enroll others to create sales.

—Matt Morris

While the previous chapter discussed ways to outsource or delegate tasks you don't want to do or aren't able to do (such as programming or graphic design), you can also outsource the most important task of all, which is advertising your business.

The number one challenge with any business is marketing. You may have the greatest product or service in the world, but if your prospective customers don't know who you are, they'll never find you.

Thus the first job of marketing is to drive customers to your business. If you fail to master marketing, your business will definitely suffer as a result.

To most businesses, marketing means advertising and hoping people will see the ads and buy their products. While that certainly is part of marketing, unless you are experienced in the art and science of advertising, it often ends up simply being an exercise in wishful thinking.

An ideal solution, which in many cases is faster, more effective, and far less expensive than buying advertising, is having others promote your business for you. I can attribute over 90 percent of the 20 million dollars-plus I've generated over the last few years to finding other marketers and companies to market my products for me in exchange for a commission. This is not to be confused with hiring a salaried sales force, but rather enrolling others as affiliates who earn commissions only if they sell something.

When I started my first Internet marketing business, I didn't know how to drive traffic to my web site. In fact, I had never marketed anything online. I read several e-books and articles about various traffic generation methods and found myself utterly and completely confused. I remember telling myself, "Matt, it can't be this hard . . . I'm a smart guy." But I knew learning all these techniques would probably take me years to master.

You can call it genius or just plain laziness, but I decided that rather than becoming a traffic generation expert, I would simply share the revenue and focus on finding others to advertise my web site by starting an affiliate program and recruiting affiliates. I knew there were literally thousands of other people who already had web sites generating huge amounts of traffic, thousands of others with large databases, and thousands of others who *were* traffic generation experts.

To start an affiliate program, also known as an associate program, you'll need to purchase an affiliate software program that will manage affiliates, track sales, and calculate commissions. Here are a few basic points on how an affiliate program works:

- An affiliate joins your program through the affiliate software sign-up page. Typically, www.yourdomain.com/affiliate or, if you have the right software and it fits with your industry, you can automatically enroll customers as affiliates and persuade them (through commissions or discounts) to refer other customers to you.

- The affiliate is given a unique web site link to advertise your site that will track all visitors generated from his or her marketing efforts.
- The affiliate software places a unique cookie on the visitor's computer so it knows which affiliate sent you the visitor.
- When the visitor makes a purchase from your web site, the affiliate software credits the appropriate affiliate, records the sale, and notifies you and the affiliate that the sale has been made.
- You send the affiliate a check at the end of the month for the sales he or she has created.

You'll want to make absolutely sure you chose the right affiliate software program. The wrong software can literally cripple your business. There are very few affiliate programs that do an effective job—I have *very* strong feelings because I estimate that I've lost well over $5 million because of choosing the wrong technology.

A few critical features to look for when selecting your affiliate program are:

- Provides click tracking for your affiliates so they know how many visitors have been sent and the number of sales created.
- Provides a marketing tools section so your affiliates can download banners, e-mails, text ads, and so forth, to be used in their marketing efforts.
- Provides proper accounting to pay your affiliates.
- Supports recurring commissions if you charge on a monthly basis versus a onetime purchase; you can pay your affiliates monthly.
- Allows reporting of top affiliates that can be used for contests.

The two solutions I recommend that have been the most consistently reliable for small businesses are:

- 1Shopping Cart (www.1ShoppingCartSoftware.com): Very inexpensive with all the basic functionality for a new business.

- InfusionSoft (www.InfusionSoftSoftware.com): More expensive but a much more robust set of features and advanced marketing tools. Currently, they even offer a guarantee that if you don't double your sales in one year, they'll refund your entire setup fee.

Both of these solutions offer an integrated e-mail program so you will not need a separate e-mail service provider.

How I Recruited Just Three Joint Venture Partners Who Earned Me over $1,000,000 Each

Here I will cover the exact strategy I followed to find and enroll other Internet marketing experts as Joint Venture partners.

Joint Venturing is really just a more elegant way to say, "You promote my web site and I'll promote yours." Or in most cases, "You become an affiliate of mine [you pay them a commission for promoting your products] and I'll become an affiliate of yours [you earn commissions for promoting their product]." The bottom line is that you're looking for other successful Internet marketers to promote your product in exchange for a commission.

Many new marketers set up their web site and order process, create an affiliate program, and then go out and try to enroll other affiliates to market their product with high hopes of having a huge army doing the work (driving traffic) for them. Typically, new marketers make one of three mistakes.

Mistake 1: Throwing mud up against the wall to see what sticks. The common misconception is that you can go out and recruit anyone and everyone to be your affiliate and that will create huge sales for you. Listen, there is nothing wrong with enrolling a ton of affiliates, but here's the rule in affiliate marketing:

Focus on QUALITY, not on QUANTITY

You can recruit thousands of affiliates but produce far fewer sales than another strategic marketer who has only five to ten affiliates. In fact, I've generated well over a million dollars in sales from only *one* of my affiliates. I'm going to cover my strategy for recruiting heavy-hitter marketers in just a moment.

Mistake 2: Not providing marketing materials for your affiliates. Here's what you'll discover about affiliates. They want as much of the work done for them as possible. If your affiliate program is selling widgets and another affiliate program is also selling widgets, affiliates are going to market the program that provides the best marketing materials for them.

Most of the affiliate software programs provide a "marketing" or "affiliate tools" section for you to upload marketing materials for your affiliates.

Before I get into mistake number three, let me cover the main marketing tools you'll need to provide.

Banners

While I almost always discourage spending money on banner advertising, you'll have many of your affiliates that will want to post them on their web sites so you definitely want to make them available. Here are a few tips on how to have your banners designed:

1. The rule of thumb for banners is that you want them to *stand out!* Don't make the mistake of creating overly professional banners that are just plain boring. With all the marketing that your prospects are bombarded with on a daily basis, you want to make sure your banners are high impact with vibrant colors.

2. Your banner should almost always be animated. Create two to three bodies of text that rotate every three to five seconds.

3. If possible, use the word *free*. People love getting something for nothing, which is why the word *free* is the most powerful word in marketing.

4. Have a call to action. Always include the words "Click Here!" or "Click Here Now!"

By far, the *best* resource I've found to create stunning, professional, and very affordable banners is through a company called Banners Mall at www.BannersMall.com.

E-mail Copy

Write three or four versions of a sales letter that affiliates can simply copy and paste, add their affiliate link (if the software doesn't do it automatically) and contact info, and put it into their e-mailing program. Also, include three or four different subject lines to choose from.

Since I simply don't have room in this book to give you all of my thoughts on how to write persuasive copy, I'll recommend a few books that have helped me tremendously.

- *Triggers* by Joe Sugarman (my favorite)
- *The Ultimate Sales Letter* by Dan Kennedy
- *How to Write a Good Advertisement* by Victor O. Schwab
- *Tested Advertising Methods* by John Caples and Fred E. Hahn

I also have some of my own personal thoughts and strategies on my web site at www.MattMorris.com/Copywriting.

Pay-Per-Click Ads for Google and Other Search Engines

One of the most powerful traffic generation strategies online is through Google Adwords, the advertising you see at the top and right side of search results in Google. For reasons beyond my understanding, many affiliate programs fail to provide text ads for their affiliates. By not providing these copy and paste text ads to your affiliates, you're missing out on potentially thousands of visitors to your site. If you provide Google ads for your affiliates, many *will* use them. Personally, I'd much prefer creating the text ads one time and letting my affiliates spend the time, energy, and money to run the ads rather than having to run them myself. I've generated thousands of sales from my affiliates over the years by having them run pay-per-click campaigns on Google and other search engines.

If you didn't read the suggestions on how to create text ads in the Internet marketing chapter, be sure to go back and read them.

Keyword Phrases for Pay-Per-Click Advertising on Google and Other Search Engines

Since you've given them the text ads to use, now you'll want to give them as many relevant keywords as possible. One of the best, and *free*, ways to generate these keywords is by using a tool Google offers for free at www.google.com/sktool.

Mistake 3: Trying to recruit top marketers without the right strategy. One of the pet peeves of top marketers is getting an e-mail from a web site owner trying to recruit them as an affiliate, or "JV partner," which is an obvious form letter.

Top marketers who can bring in hundreds or thousands of customers to you will almost never respond to a form letter. In fact, not only will they not respond, they'll make a mental note of your name as someone they don't want to be bothered by.

The other pet peeve is getting a letter, even if it's personal, that is one-sided—meaning the web site owner wants the top marketer to promote his or her product because of the huge sums of money he or she can make without wanting to promote the top marketer in return.

Here's how that letter might look (a good example of what *not* to do):

Hi John,

My name is Stan and I've developed the most revolutionary Widget that has ever been created. The product is so amazing it practically sells itself. I'd like to have you as one of my joint venture partners. I'm paying a 70 percent commission to my affiliates. Because I know you are a top marketer, I know you'll make a TON of money by promoting my products!

Here's my web site, www.stantheidiot.com, and you can sign up as an affiliate at the bottom of the page.

Feel free to call me if you have any questions,

Stan T. Idiot
(888) 555-1212

Tune in to WIIFM

Remember, the one and only station your prospects are tuned into is WIIFM—"What's in it for me?" In most cases, top marketers have their own products on the market. Typically, they are much more interested in selling their own products, rather than marketing someone else's. They *will* often promote others, but they want you to promote them in return. I'll give you a much better example of a letter to write in just a moment, but first, I want to give you the exact strategy I used to attract several top marketers, three of which have generated well over $1 million each for my businesses.

Formula for Recruiting Joint Venture Partners

Note: This is a perfect project for a virtual assistant. See Chapter 13 for details.

Step 1: Create a Joint Venture spreadsheet.
Open an Excel Spreadsheet that looks like this:

Web Site	Alexa Rank	Owner	Phone	E-Mail	Notes

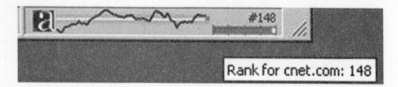

FIGURE 14.1   The Alexa Toolbar Instantly Displays the Ranking of Any
Web Site You Visit

Step 2: Download the Alexa Toolbar. If you're going to recruit joint venture partners, one of the most effective ways to do that is to recruit web site owners in your niche who get a lot of traffic on their web site. The web site www.Alexa.com measures and ranks web sites by number, which is called the web site's traffic rank. A number one ranking would be the number one most visited web site on the Internet, while a number ten ranking would be the tenth most visited web site.

Alexa allows you to download a free toolbar that works with popular browsers such as Internet Explorer and Firefox. When you visit a web site, your Alexa toolbar will instantly give you the ranking of that web site, as seen in Figure 14.1. Alexa will also give you "related links," which are web sites similar to the one you are currently viewing— another useful tool in this process.

Step 3: Begin searching Google for sites in your niche. If your business sells dog grooming brushes and you wanted to find other web sites that sell similar products, you could search for "dog grooming products" or any other relevant term and see which sites Google finds for you.

When your search listings pull up, a great source of top web sites are the "sponsored links," which appear at the top and right side of your search results (as shown in Figure 14.2). Sponsored links are web sites that are paying for placement, and in many cases are a great way to find web sites that get a lot of traffic in your niche.

Certainly do not limit yourself to just the sponsored links. The first one to three pages of organic listings, which are the nonsponsored links, can be just as good a resource for finding high-trafficked web sites.

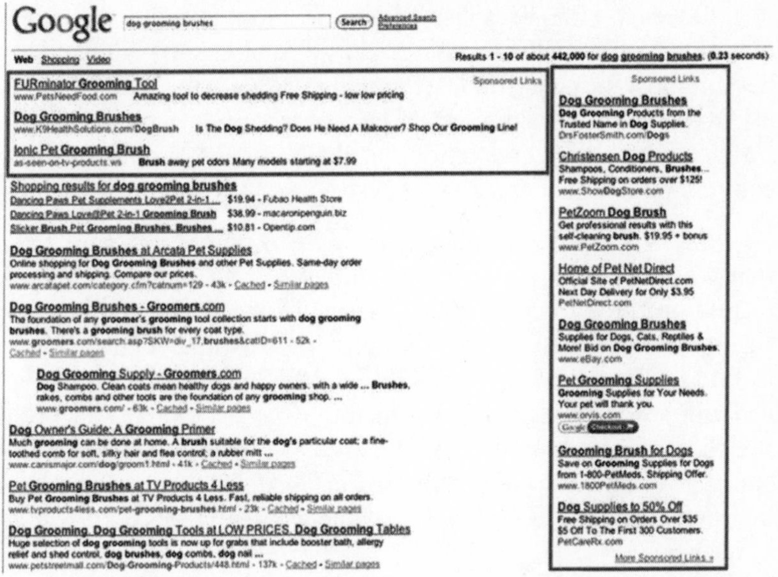

FIGURE 14.2   Sponsored Links on Google Identify Potentially High-Traffic Web Sites

Simply click on each page and check its traffic ranking on your Alexa toolbar. My criterion when I first got started was to find web sites that were in the top 50,000 of all web sites online. Depending on the competition in your niche, you could expand that to 100,000 or lower it to 30,000 or less. Once you find a web site meeting your criteria, put the web site and its Alexa rank in your spreadsheet. Once you find a highly trafficked web site, you can also use the "related links" feature to find other sites that are similar and may meet your criteria for your database.

Web Site	Alexa Rank	Owner	Phone	E-Mail	Notes
www.abcsite.com	45,292				
www.defsite.com	28,388				

Once you target a list of all the most popular web sites that could potentially promote your web site, sort them in order of most popular to least popular. This can be done easily in Excel by clicking the Data Menu and then using the sort feature to sort in ascending order based on the Alexa Rank column.

Step 4: Find the owners of these highly trafficked web sites. Now that you have your list of highly trafficked web sites, you'll want to find out how to contact the owner of each site. Very few web sites post the actual owner's contact information. The best way to find this out is to do what's called a "WhoIs" lookup (see Figure 14.3), which identifies the name, e-mail address, and often the direct phone number of the web site owner. One popular site that lets you do a WhoIs lookup is WhoIs.net (www.whois .net) or Network Solutions (www.networksolutions.com/whois/ index.jsp).

Once you find the name, address, and phone number of each web site owner, type that information into your spreadsheet.

Web Site	Alexa Rank	Owner	Phone	E-Mail	Notes
www.abcsite.com	45,292	John Doe	888-555-1212	john@doe.com	
www.defsite.com	28,388	Sue Smith	888-555-2121	sue@smith.com	

Step 5: Contact the web site owner to request joint venture. When you contact the web site owner, introduce yourself and offer a possible joint venture that could be of mutual benefit. (Notice the word "mutual.")

My success in obtaining successful joint venture relationships came not just by sending the owner a personal e-mail, but from doing what hardly any other Internet marketers do—actually *calling* them on the phone.

I'll cover the e-mail first.

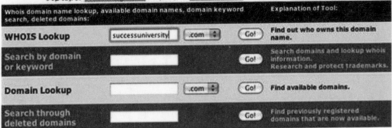

FIGURE 14.3   A WhoIs Lookup Can Identify the Owner of a
Web Site Domain

Keep in mind that many successful Internet marketers are bombarded with requests for them to promote other products, so it's key to be different than all the other form letter e-mails they receive. If they have even a hint that your e-mail is a form letter or spam, you'll get automatically deleted.

The most important part of the e-mail is the subject line because the subject line alone will determine if they open the e-mail or not. If the subject line looks like spam, they most certainly will not open your e-mail. The key is to be personal without any hype whatsoever.

Here are a couple examples I've used with great success:

Subject Line Example 1: To JOHN from MATT

This subject line is incredibly simple, but has been amazingly effective for me. Because his name is in all caps, it will tend to grab his attention and it's completely personal.

Subject Line Example 2: John, I'd like to promote your (insert name of his product)

This subject line is completely benefits-driven and is letting him know even before he opens the e-mail that I want to do something for him. It's a perfect example of tuning in to WIIFM ("What's in it for me?").

Next, you'll want to craft a personal e-mail introducing yourself and explaining *quickly* what you are proposing. *Warning*: Do *not* send e-mails through an auto-responder with a remove link at the bottom. He or she will automatically assume it is spam.

Here's an example of a possible e-mail (I'll use dog grooming as an example niche):

Hi John,

I love your web site!

I also market dog grooming supplies and am the owner of www. abcDogGrooming.com.

Because we're in the same niche, and your product seems to be superb, I'd love to promote your web site in exchange for a cross-promotion.

I'm more than happy to send you a complimentary copy of my product if you're interested in working together. Our affiliates earn $xx per sale from each product sold from my site, which converts extremely well. You can read all the details on my affiliate program at www.abdDogGrooming.com/affiliate.

I can have my assistant sign you up as an affiliate and send you our promo materials when you're ready. My direct line is (888) 555-1212 or you can e-mail me your phone number if you'd like to have a quick chat.

Please let me know if you would like to work together and I'll look forward to a long and prosperous relationship!

Warm regards,
Joe Miller
Founder, ABC Dog Grooming
joe@abcDogGrooming.com
(888) 555-1212

This is obviously a very basic example. It's always a good idea to reference any personal information you know about him or her, such as the person's background, location, similarities, and so forth. If you have any other big name marketers you're working with or any other highly trafficked web sites that promote your products, certainly include them in the e-mail as examples of social proof.

If your first e-mail doesn't get a response, definitely write a few to send to him or her afterward to follow up. You might even consider sending a traditional letter through the postal system. Here's another example of an e-mail I've used effectively that explains exactly how I'd like to promote the marketer's products and what I'm looking for in return.

Hi John,

I'd like to discuss marketing your products to all of my customers.

(continued)

I own the web site www.abcDogGrooming.com and am looking for three to five integration marketing partners who I will be promoting to all my customers.

Here's what I'll do . . .

After my customer makes his or her purchase, I'll send out an e-mail every five to seven days promoting complimentary products in the dog grooming niche. I'll promote each marketing partner two to three times to each of my customers. Your product looks superb and seems to be a perfect fit.

In exchange for promoting your products, I'll just ask that you give me an equal number of reciprocal mailings. I'm more than happy to send you a complimentary copy of my product if you're interested in working together. You'll earn $xx per sale from each product sold from my site, which converts extremely well. You can read all the details on my affiliate program at www.abcDogGrooming.com/affiliate.

I can have my assistant sign you up as an affiliate and send you our promo materials when you're ready. My direct line is (888) 555-1212 or you can e-mail me your phone number if you'd like to have a quick chat.

Please let me know if you would like to work together and I'll look forward to a long and prosperous relationship!

Warm regards,
Joe Miller
Founder, ABC Dog Grooming
joe@abcDogGrooming.com
(888) 555-1212

Remember, this is a numbers game. You'll want to contact a *lot* of different web site owners to begin developing these relationships and send them several personal e-mails to get their attention.

Next, you'll want to begin calling each of these web site owners to introduce yourself over the phone. When you make a personal call, you're so much more likely to develop joint venture partners for a couple of reasons.

First, you're establishing trust and rapport because you're not hiding behind your computer. By establishing a friendship over the phone, you're a lot more likely to develop a long term business relationship with that web site owner.

Second, you're getting that owner's attention. You may not get a call back, but he or she is a lot more likely now to open your e-mails.

Here's an example of a message you might leave:

Hi John, this is Joe Smith with abcDogGrooming.com. I came across your web site and love what you're doing. I just sent you an e-mail and would like to discuss promoting your product through my integration marketing program. I can be reached at 888-555-1212 or you can e-mail me at joe@smith.com Have a great day.

When I first got started online, I went through this process with about 200 different web site owners. For the most part, I got little to no response from my e-mails and calls. But out of those 200, I ended up working with those three different marketers I mentioned earlier who have been responsible for bringing my companies well over one million dollars *each!*

The Gold Is in the Relationship

The key to retaining the best people in any business is rewarding and recognizing them. Most businesses reward their partners with cash, but people will actually do more for recognition and relationships than for money. All things being equal, more people will choose to work with you above the competition if you've built a strong relationship with your partners.

Earlier I mentioned how I would contact the top web sites in my niche and start a dialogue about working together. Even if someone does not want to work with you, stay in contact with him or her anyway. My theory is that every time someone tells me, "No," that really just means, "Not yet."

Mail the person samples of your product to remind him or her of who you are and what your company does. Then send the person cards for every holiday such as Christmas, Valentine's Day, or even a birthday (if you can find out his or her birthday).

I consistently send special gifts on occasions to my key partners and affiliates above and beyond the commission checks they receive. I'll send flowers, gift baskets, or anything creative that will build our relationship.

About a year ago, I was on the phone with one of my top affiliates who told me about her New Year's resolutions. In our conversation, she casually mentioned that she had gone to a particular store to look at treadmills so she could start working out at home. After I got off the phone, I called that store and bought a gift card that was enough to cover one of their most expensive models and had the store mail it to her from me. I still remember the thank you call I received and how she just couldn't believe what I did for her. The few hundred dollars spent on the treadmill was peanuts compared to the hundreds of thousands of dollars she has generated for my company. Not only do things like this come back to you in monetary rewards, the personal feeling of being able to put a smile on someone's face is an even better reward than the money.

How I Turned $70 into $15,000 in Less than Six Months

A couple of years ago, I had the opportunity to meet a multimillion dollar Internet marketer who I wanted to do business with. I had requested that he promote my company and for whatever reason, he never moved forward with doing so. Rather than count him out, I added him to my influencer list so I could stay in regular contact.

A few months after meeting him, I received an e-mail that he sent to his entire database announcing that he and his wife just had a baby. I called his office to get his personal address and had roses sent to his house to congratulate him and his wife.

Not only did I get an e-mail back from him saying how much he appreciated it, soon after that, he rolled out a $15,000 private mastermind group that he invited me to attend for free. I guarantee he never would have thought of inviting me if I hadn't sent his family $70 worth of flowers after she gave birth.

When you do business with people, send handwritten thank-you notes. When you talk with someone over the phone, send a quick note that says something like, "Enjoyed talking to you yesterday. Let me know if I can help you in any way with your new project."

Handwritten notes make you stand out among the crowd of marketers vying for the attention of businesspeople. When you've sent samples of your products, gifts, or even just handwritten cards to potential partners, your name will have top of mind awareness. And because your name is on their mind, you're more likely to get the call when a potential partnership opportunity comes up.

Start Identifying Potential Joint Partners

In business, you can do all the work yourself or you can let someone else do the work and you still reap the benefits. By recruiting others to help you out while you help them out, you can reach new customers with very little effort.

So get started today. Identify your potential partners, use the sample e-mail letters to contact related businesses, and make sure you're prepared to handle a flood of customers because, as I've experienced, they often come much faster than you expect.

15

Five Specific Strategies to Crush the Competition

Are you green and growing or ripe and rotting?

—Ray Kroc

Every business is going to have competition. For your business to survive, you'll need a consistent strategy for dealing with competition. Competition will always be there. Your goal is to position your business to negate the competition's advantages and drive more potential customers to your business instead.

To achieve this goal, here are five different strategies to consider. You may only need one of them, or you may want to use several in combination or separately at different times.

Strategy 1: Offer a Lower Price

Often companies in the marketplace are overpriced simply because there are few competitors. A perfect example of this occurred with the long-distance calling industry. Back in the early 1990s there were only three companies with a monopoly in the long-distance industry: AT&T, MCI, and Sprint. Since they had no competition, they could easily charge $0.25 per minute or more until competitors forced them to lower prices or risk losing customers.

Wal-Mart is a perfect example of how lowering prices can drive most competitors out of business. However, the danger of just lowering prices is that you can get into a price war where the largest company with the biggest cash reserves will win.

If you really want to drive your competitors crazy, try forcing them to compete against a free product. You'll of course need to be able to have a product that you can afford to give away free in exchange for making up the revenue on charging for something else.

To see how a free product makes it difficult for a competitor to compete, consider the war between Apple and Microsoft. Both sell operating systems, which are the programs that make your computer work. Beyond superficial differences, Microsoft Windows and Apple's Mac OS X basically offer similar features. However, the key difference is that every copy of Apple's Mac OS X comes with a suite of free programs dubbed iLife.

One of the most popular programs in this iLife suite is iPhoto, a program that makes it easy and fun to organize and manage photographs captured through your digital camera. Given a choice between using Microsoft Windows and having to buy a separate digital photograph program or getting it for free with every Apple computer, many consumers choose Apple for the "free" iPhoto program.

Microsoft later came out with its own free digital photograph organizing program, dubbed Windows Photo Gallery, which has actually gotten better reviews than iPhoto. However, since Apple released iPhoto first, it has imprinted the idea that storing and organizing digital photographs is far easier with Apple software than Microsoft. To this day, iPhoto and the rest of the free iLlife suite continue to help sell Apple computers.

Just remember that lowering your price should never be your sole solution. When you compete on price alone, someone can always offer lower prices and eventually shave your profit margins down to zero. A better solution might be selective price cutting.

Amazon.com does this brilliantly with its huge discounts on books. Then to sweeten the deal, they'll offer free shipping on orders $25 and higher. Traditional brick and mortar bookstores can't compete on price alone since Amazon.com can always undercut them. Instead, the larger bookstore chains are now competing selectively.

Rather than lower the prices on all of their books, bookstores are exploiting their advantage of immediate gratification. No matter how much money you save buying books through Amazon.com, you have to wait for your books through the mail. You could pay more to get your books shipped overnight, but that defeats the price advantage of Amazon.com in the first place.

These major bookstore chains now offer discount coupons for either one book or your entire purchase of books. You still get a discount, but you also get immediate gratification by not having to wait for the book by mail.

Use lower prices selectively and consider a way to offer a free product that will force your competitors to scramble to keep up with you. Unless you're a big company with plenty of cash reserves, you probably can't afford wholesale price cutting. However, you can thrive with selective price cutting, which can attract customers while keeping your profit margins healthy at the same time.

Strategy 2: Ethical Bribery

This one concept alone has been responsible for increasing my conversion rates by over 500 percent when selling online. An ethical bribe is giving your prospect something extra as an incentive to buy right now.

Since people always want to believe they are getting the best deal possible, offering bonuses will greatly increase the perceived value of any purchase decision. You may have noticed an "ethical" bribe when you made the decision to purchase this book. On the cover of this book is a bonus offer to receive a series of *free* downloadable CDs I recorded in interviews with other Millionaire Entrepreneurs, valued at $97. This is a great example of a good bonus because there is an extremely high perceived value for these downloadable CDs, but the only thing it cost me to record them was the cost of the conference recording service and my time and effort.

A bonus is anything you can add to the purchase to sweeten the deal. You'll want to get creative with your bonuses and find one or more low cost, or no cost, but high perceived value offerings, that you can give away at no additional cost to the customer. My favorite bonus is information, which may be an mp3 audio file that essentially costs you nothing to store or duplicate, but provides valuable information in the eyes of the customer. You can also create a free report, saved as a PDF file, that you can give away as an e-book, which again costs you nothing to deliver by e-mail or as a download on your web site.

The key is finding something that fits with the product you're selling. Be careful not to offer a bonus that has nothing to do with your product. If you're selling gardening supplies, you might give away a special report on how to beautify your garden, how to reduce weeds without using pesticides, or how to grow the biggest fruits in your neighborhood, but you wouldn't offer tips on car repair.

Be sure to always establish a value for your bonuses. Price it at $9.95, $29, $97—whatever is consistent with what you're selling. Whatever you do, do not overinflate the value because it will cause you to lose credibility with your prospect.

If you write a special report valued at $1,000, you may actually believe the information in the report is worth that much, but it's completely inconsistent with what most e-books or books in the bookstore sell for, and your prospects will be too skeptical to do business with you.

Why do bonuses work so well?

One of the most powerful words in marketing is the word *free*. We all love to receive something for *free!*

The Power of *Free!*

One of the most powerful examples of the power of free is explained in Dan Ariely's book, *Predictably Irrational.*

Dan and two of his colleagues set up a table at a large public building and offered two kinds of chocolates—Lindt truffles and Hershey's Kisses. There was a large sign above the table that read, "One chocolate per customer."

For those of you who are not chocolate connoisseurs, Lindt is produced by a Swiss firm that has been blending fine cocoas for 160 years. Lindt's chocolate truffles are particularly prized—exquisitely creamy and just about irresistible. They cost about 30 cents each when we buy them in bulk. Hershey's Kisses, on the other hand, are good little chocolates, but let's face it, they are rather ordinary.

So what happened when the "customers" flocked to our table? When we set the price of a Lindt truffle at 15 cents and a Kiss at one cent, we were not surprised to find that our customers acted with a good deal of rationality: They compared the price and quality of the Kiss with the price and quality of the truffle, and then made their choice. About 73 percent of them chose the truffle and 27 percent chose a Kiss.

Now we decided to see what a difference *"free!"* might make in the situation. So we offered the Lindt truffle for 14 cents and the Kisses for free. Would there be a difference? Should there be? After all, we had merely lowered the price of both kinds of chocolates by one cent.

But what a difference *"free!"* made. The humble Hershey's Kiss became a big favorite. Some 69 percent of our customers (up from 27 percent before) chose the free Kiss. The Lindt truffle took a tumble; customers choosing it decreased from 73 to 31 percent!

If you look at almost every infomercial on television, it always has a call to action that says something like, "If you call within the next five minutes, you'll receive an extra set of knives completely FREE!"

Any time you give away a bonus gift for making a purchase, customers feel they're getting more for their money. Combine this with the warning that they'll only get this free bonus gift *if* they act right now and you can prod customers into ordering right away. If you always give customers more than what they pay for, they'll always be happy. Happy customers tell their friends, which increases the chance of turning customers into unpaid salespeople.

The Law of Reciprocity

One of the most powerful psychological triggers in marketing is the law of reciprocity. This law states that when we have been given a gift, we feel an overriding sense of obligation to repay that gift.

The Hare Krishnas, a highly publicized religious group prevalent in the 1960s and 1970s with shaved heads, wearing oversized robes, beads, and bells, regularly roamed airports and other public places asking for donations. Most people avoided them, a small handful listened to them, and a tiny percentage bothered to give them money.

To increase their chances of success, the Hare Krishnas implemented a new marketing strategy. They began cheerfully giving passersby a small flower before that person had a chance to reject them. After saying "it is our gift to you," they would then ask for a small donation. Because they had already received something first as a gift, most people felt obligated to donate a small fee in return, as payment for the flower.

After paying, many people simply threw the flower away in the first trash can they could find. The Hare Krishnas would dig these flowers out of the trash and hand them

(continued)

out to a new batch of "customers." By virtue of the law of reciprocity, the Hare Krishnas significantly increased the amount of donations they received, even though most people never even kept, let alone wanted, the flowers.

Try applying this Hare Krishna marketing technique in your own business. Before you expect customers to buy anything, give them something first. This initial free product can be information or a token gift, but it needs to be something with perceived value. By the simple act of giving, you may be surprised at how much you'll actually get in return.

Strategy 3: Offer Higher Levels of Personalized Service

There's a big difference between Wal-Mart and Nordstrom. Wal-Mart specializes in low prices for basic goods. Nordstrom specializes in luxury items at higher prices. Yet both businesses remain profitable.

The key to Wal-Mart is low prices. The key to Nordstrom is superior service. Walk into any Nordstrom and you can buy quality merchandise with superior service and a quality guarantee. If you need to return a product for any reason, just bring it back and get your money back. They don't advertise this (I think they should) but there is no time limit on the guarantee, which makes Nordstrom my favorite clothing retailer. Because I know I can return any product I purchase anytime if there is a defect in quality, I buy the majority of my clothes and shoes there. I've spent thousands upon thousands of dollars at Nordstrom's for that reason alone. And in all the years I've been shopping there, I've only returned one pair of shoes.

I purchased a pair of dress shoes that I wore for about a month. I loved the look of the shoes but they hurt my feet to the point where I stopped wearing them. About a week later, I told my wife I should put their guarantee to the test and go return them and get my money back. She thought I was crazy because surely they wouldn't allow a return on a pair of shoes I wore for a month! Well,

I walked right in, explained to the clerk that these shoes really hurt my feet and that I simply couldn't wear them and requested my money back. Without a second thought, the clerk processed my refund and put the money back on my credit card—simple as that!

I can guarantee that one return has earned Nordstrom a lot more business than the cost of those shoes. Not only did that experience even further build my loyalty—causing me to purchase more from that company— I've told that story to countless others who have no doubt purchased from it as well.

The personal computer market offers another example of how superior service can translate into a competitive advantage. Most computers are sold by a variety of manufacturers with a bewildering array of options and features. Sorting out the best computer to buy can be difficult, and once you buy a computer, trying to get help using or repairing it can be another headache.

Now walk into any Apple Store and you'll see computers available for you to examine and try. More importantly, Apple offers service. If you have an old PC and buy a Macintosh, the Apple Store will transfer the data off your old computer and put it on your new Macintosh for free. If you have trouble learning to use your computer, you can sign up for additional classes in a group setting or with private one-on-one tutoring.

By taking the headache out of buying, shopping, repairing, and learning to use a computer, Apple has gained a competitive advantage that even a competitor like Hewlett-Packard or Dell Computers can't hope to match. Given a choice between service and price, some people may prefer price while others prefer service. If you compete on price alone, you'll always be cutting your own profit margins, but if you compete on service alone, your competitors will have a hard time competing against you. Plus you'll be able to keep your profit margins healthy and deal with a more loyal base of customers.

Strategy 4: Put Your Money Where Your Mouth Is

As I'm sure you know from your own experience, it's simply human nature to be a little bit skeptical when you make buying decisions. If a consumer can choose between you and your competitor, assuming everything else is equal, he or she will typically choose the product or service with the best guarantee.

One of the best strategies for increasing your sales is offering a guarantee that makes buying from you a no-brainer decision. If a customer is unhappy with your product or service, your guarantee makes it easy for customers to get their money back. That makes buying from you a risk-free decision.

Guarantees show the customer that you have enough faith in your product (or service) that you're willing to shoulder the risk of the transaction. This is what is called *risk reversal*.

When crafting your guarantee, it's important that the guarantee is done in a way that eliminates any doubt of having to jump through hoops to get money back. What a consumer ultimately wants is an *ironclad* guarantee without any fine print. Make your guarantee plain and simple so there's no guesswork.

The best wording I've used for a guarantee was learned from Bill Harris and Brad Antin from Centerpointe Research Institute (www.CenterPointe.com). These guys are marketing geniuses, so I would highly advise going to their web site to see many of these techniques being used.

Here's an example of a great guarantee:

If, after you purchase this product, you feel for any reason it fails to live up to our promises (or even if it does and you just change your mind), simply return it and we'll immediately and cheerfully give you a 100 percent refund—no questions asked!

Notice the statement in parenthesis in the guarantee. This is inserted because of another factor that plays into the psychology of your prospects. They may trust you 100 percent, but may still be unhappy with the product even if it performs as advertised. Buyers may simply be unhappy with their purchase decision, which is known as buyer's remorse. By addressing the possibility of buyer's remorse, your guarantee eliminates any perceived risk.

The risk with any comprehensive guarantee is that some people will take advantage of it and rip you off. However, the number of people willing to rip you off will almost always be much lower than the additional number of people your guarantee will attract. Based on my experience selling over $20 million worth of products and services online, I can tell you that it's a very small percentage.

When that happens, simply consider that a cost of doing business. In fact, most large direct response infomercial companies factor in as much as 10 to 20 percent of their revenue as refunds. Their philosophy is that if they're not getting a decent number of refunds, it means they're not selling hard enough.

In most cases, for every dollar this guarantee strategy costs you because of someone taking advantage of you, you'll make $5 or $10 dollars in profit from the additional sales it generates. Even if you absolutely know someone is taking advantage of you, it's better to honor your guarantee than risk any negative publicity. One negative complaint posted in a blog or forum online can spur complaints from dozens of others and prevent prospects from buying your products after reading these negative posts. In my company, we'll even refund someone *after* the guarantee has passed by because we simply do not want any negative publicity.

This brings up the next question. How long should I offer a refund?

The answer is that there really aren't any hard and fast rules on the length of the guarantee. The best advice I can give is to make your guarantee longer than your competitor's. If your prospect is looking at your product versus your competitor's, with all else being the same, they're going to choose the product with the longest guarantee.

Giving a long guarantee worries many business owners, but there are two reasons you shouldn't be too concerned. First, if your product or service is really good, it shouldn't give you any problems because believe it or not, most people are genuinely good at heart and are not going to cheat you. The people who are going to cheat you are typically going to do it very quickly anyway.

The second reason has more to do with psychology that may seem a bit counterintuitive. In general, the longer people have to do something, the greater the likelihood that they'll forget to do it!

If you sell something with a short-term guarantee, the buyer will feel pressured to make a quick decision to return the product right away if necessary. If he or she is teetering on keeping it versus returning it, the buyer will usually return it because he or she knows the window of opportunity is about to expire.

If you use a long-term guarantee like a one-year, three-year, or even a lifetime guarantee, that pressure to make a quick decision completely goes away. Now, the buyer has the luxury of having plenty of time to make that decision, and in most cases will simply forget about making the decision at all and keep the product.

Another powerful strategy is making a guarantee so that your customer will actually benefit even if he or she does return your product. As I mentioned earlier, it's a wise decision to offer special bonuses with your product.

You can reverse the risk completely by allowing your customer to keep the bonus gifts even if he or she returns the product for a full refund. If you've established a value for your bonuses, your prospect will calculate the total value of what he or she will end up keeping even if he or she doesn't keep the original product. When the customer sees that the value of the bonuses alone are almost as much, or even more, than the cost of the product, it's a winning situation even if the product is returned.

Your guarantee might read something like this:

If, after you purchase this product, you feel, for any reason, it fails to live up to our promises (or even if it does and you just change your mind), simply return it and we'll immediately and cheerfully give you a 100 percent refund—no questions asked!

Even if you decide to return this product for a full refund, please keep the FREE Bonus(es) as our special gift to you as our way of saying thank you for at least giving us a try! So even if you decide that our product is not right for you, you'll get a $xx value absolutely FREE. That's BETTER THAN RISK FREE!

Warning! This next strategy is not for the faint of heart. It should be tested on a small scale first before being rolled out on a larger scale.

This is a strategy that I've used on a few occasions when I'm marketing to a small group of existing customers only. I've heard marketers use this for the general public before with great success, but because my company does business all around the world, and certain countries have a high degree of fraud, I've only done it on a limited scale.

Rather than just offer an ordinary 100 percent money-back guarantee, offer a "more than your money back guarantee" like this:

*We're SO confident in our product that if you feel, for any reason, it fails to live up to our promises, simply return it and we'll immediately and cheerfully give you a **150 percent refund!***

*You'll also get to keep the FREE Bonuses as our special gift to you as our way of saying thank you for at least giving us a try! So even if you decide that our product is not right for you, the worst case scenario is that you'll end up with **MORE THAN YOUR MONEY BACK!***

An offer like that is almost impossible for a qualified prospect to ignore and will definitely put you light years ahead of your competition. Notice that I *did* take off "no questions asked" to at least slightly lower the risk.

This is a strategy that I advise when selling additional products to customers who have already established a record of trust. You trust them based on past purchases that they won't cheat you and they trust you'll honor your word because you delivered a product of solid value to them in the past.

This element of trust is an absolute requirement when offering a guarantee, which is further explained in strategy 5.

Strategy 5: Establish Greater Levels of Trust

We typically prefer to do business with people we like and trust, don't we? You can offer all the guarantees in the world, but if you haven't established trust in the mind of your prospect, the guarantee becomes worthless because the person doesn't have faith that you'll honor it.

So even when your product or service is great, well-priced with bonuses and guarantees, there is one major element standing in the way of the sale—a lack of trust.

Like it or not, people are trained to be skeptical. They are conditioned to *not* believe you.

What we'll cover in this section is a number of psychological triggers that will help to create trust between you and your prospects. Here are a few key elements that you'll want to consider including in your advertising.

Social Proof

Social proof is a phenomenon that occurs in ambiguous social situations when people are unable to determine the appropriate mode of behavior on their own. In these situations, the answer lies in learning from the actions of others to make a decision.

This is a psychological trigger that's built into all of us and one that's been around as long as the human race. In short, we make decisions based on what we see other people doing.

Social proof is a shortcut that allows us to turn off the thousands of little decisions we have to make every day. We tend to follow what others are doing in situations where we're not 100 percent certain ourselves.

If you've ever come off an airplane to walk to baggage claim, you may have found yourself there without ever looking at the signs leading to it. Instead, you simply followed the crowd of people who got off the plane ahead of you. Social proof essentially says that we determine what is correct by finding out what other people think is correct.

Perhaps the best way to utilize social proof in your marketing can be done by showcasing your happy customers.

Testimonials

It's easy for a seller to boast and brag about the virtues of his product, but no matter what you say, potential buyers will always remain skeptical. After all, they expect *you* to boast about your product or service.

However, your customer's boasts about your product or service lends greater credibility. First of all, customers aren't being paid to praise your business. Second, out of dozens of happy customers, maybe only one will actually take the time to write a letter praising your business. For every testimonial you receive and display, chances are good, in the minds of your prospects, that countless other happy customers feel the same way about your business.

Even more powerful are testimonials from respected community members. Seeing a testimonial from another person can build your credibility, but seeing a testimonial from a prominent politician or celebrity can shoot your credibility through the roof. In this case, your business benefits from its association with the respected person giving the testimonial.

If you were looking for cookware, what would be more convincing? A testimonial from a stay-at-home dad in New Hampshire or a testimonial from a world-renowned chef who currently hosts her own cooking show every week on the Food Network?

What gives testimonials even greater credibility is seeing pictures of the person, which helps potential customers see that a real person wrote the testimonial. Even more powerful are testimonials that include an audio or video clip of the person raving about your business.

The key to testimonials is believability. If customers can see people, much like themselves, raving about a business, they'll place more trust in your business as a result. List a person's full name and location along with a picture, video, and a short testimonial, and this will greater establish your credibility as a business.

When you're first launching your business or product, you won't have any customers, so the quickest way to get testimonials is to give your product away for free. Then solicit feedback from these early testers and use their positive remarks as testimonials. Now when you're ready to launch your product, you'll already have a handful of legitimate testimonials to help market your product or business.

The Bandwagon Effect

Another powerful social proof element can be found in what's called the "bandwagon" effect. The general rule is that conduct or beliefs spread among people with the probability of any individual adopting it increasing with the proportion who have already done so. In other words, the more people do something, the more others also "hop on the bandwagon" and do so as well. Business tends to attract more business.

If you've had an impressive number of people purchase your product, then without a doubt, state that number. With my company, Success University, we've enrolled approximately 100,000 students in 180 countries around the world. That's an impressive number, which, in the minds of our prospects, says that "if that many people have done it, it must be a good thing."

You could also include the ranking of your web site in your particular industry. If you're in a small industry, such as dog grooming, you might be able to state that your web site is the most popular dog grooming web site online, according to Alexa.com or Ranking.com. In our first year in business, for example, we initiated a huge online marketing campaign and become the number one most visited personal development web site online. That provided so much credibility for us in our industry that we used it as a major factor to more than quadruple our sales the following year.

Besides testimonials, here are five more ways to build trust in your business through the customer's eyes when you are marketing online:

1. *Credibility Seals*: A credibility seal promotes your business through an independent third party. The most common credibility seal is a symbol from the Better Business Bureau, which helps to establish your business as trustworthy. On the Internet, there are a number of different seals that you can post on your web site once you pass their application process. Here are a few for you to check out:

- Verisign (www.verisign.com)
- Truste (www.truste.org)
- McAfee Secure (www.mcafeesecure.com/us)
- BBB Online (www.bbb.org/online)

In almost every case, adding two or three of these seals will increase sales conversions on your web site.

2. *Privacy Policy:* If you collect any information from visitors on your web site (and every web site should), you need to display a privacy policy that explains what you will and will not do with their contact information. A link to this privacy policy should be easily found on your web site. Any prominently displayed privacy policy will ease people's fears that their information will not be abused in any way.

3. *Your Picture:* If it's at all reasonable in your industry, include your picture for customers to see. By including a professional photograph of yourself, you establish credibility by the simple fact that you're not trying to hide behind the Internet. People buy from people they know and trust. When you're not a big name corporation, having your picture posted on your web site automatically lends credibility. Your smiling face is the best way to establish that connection.

It's one of the cornerstone elements in the real estate industry. You've probably noticed that most successful real estate agents include their picture on their business cards, brochures, and some even on the yard signs. These agents understand the importance of branding yourself to establish trust.

4. *Your Signature:* Any time you're writing a sales letter, whether it's on the Web, direct mail, or even on a brochure, my testing has always found that letters with a real signature translate into more sales than an identical letter without a signature. To put your signature on the web, you'll just need to scan in your signature, convert it to a .jpg image, and have your webmaster put it on your web site.

5. *Your Company's Contact Details:* Always include your name or company name, address, and telephone number. One of the biggest mistakes online marketers make is thinking that someone will make a purchase when he or she can't see how to contact you. Some business owners worry that they will get inundated with calls from prospects, but in reality, very few will ever call. Your prospect just wants the reassurance that if something goes wrong he or she will know how to get in touch with you. If you're worried about privacy you can always get an answering service or a voice mail box to take the calls.

Become an Expert

A final way to establish credibility is to become known as an expert, and the fastest way to be known as an expert is to write a book or article, or appear on radio or TV. Let's start with the simplest method first.

Write Articles

Everybody knows something more than other people. If you're in a business you're totally passionate about, you already possess information that most people will never have. To present yourself as an expert, write articles.

These articles can be short. They just need to be published or distributed somewhere. One popular site to post articles is Ezine Articles (http://EzineArticles.com). Just write an article, post it on the web site, and other businesses that have newsletters will turn to Ezine Articles to look for relevant articles to publish. At the end of each article, write a biography about who you are, what your business is, and how to contact you. Now when people see your article published in a newsletter, you'll establish credibility as an expert in that field.

Look in your community newspaper and you'll find stockbrokers, financial planners, and real estate agents who write short columns loaded with advice for buying stocks, managing your money, or selling a home. By constantly publishing such columns every month, these people establish themselves as experts in their field. (If you can't write, don't worry. You can often hire ghostwriters to do the work for you.)

Getting your article printed in an ezine or business newsletter is often enough to establish credibility, but if possible, consider getting an article printed in a magazine. Every industry has its own specialized magazines. If you can get an article published, you'll establish instant credibility with both customers and your competition.

Become an Author

By far, the strongest credibility factor you can possibly have in your favor is being the author of a book. As an author, you can use your book to brand yourself as an expert and use your book as the ultimate business card. Being an author garners immediate credibility and establishes an infinitely higher level of respect than any competitor without that status. If you're interested in the easiest way to become an author, you can visit my web site to learn how to apply as a coauthor in my next book. Go to www.MattMorris.com/BeAnAuthor to see if you qualify.

Get on TV or Radio

Don't overlook radio or TV either. Contact your local radio and TV stations to let them know you'd be willing to speak and be interviewed about different subjects. If a flood, tornado, or other natural disaster strikes your area, call a radio and TV station to let the station know you'd be willing to chat about the disaster from your unique expertise. For example, insurance agents can discuss the types of insurance people should have to protect themselves from such disasters while veterinarians can talk about how to keep your pet safe in an emergency and how to prepare ahead of time. Such an interview can establish massive credibility for you and your business.

The fact is that if you can author an article or book, or appear on radio or TV, the public will associate you with success and trust you more. After all, if a magazine publisher, or radio and TV station trusted you, other people have no reason not to trust you too.

Go Out and Crush Your Competition

Crushing your competition means knowing your competition's strengths and weaknesses, knowing your own strengths and weaknesses, and exploiting both to your advantage. There will always be a certain segment of the population who will always choose your competitors, but you want to target those people who are undecided.

By using one or more of these five strategies, you can crush your competition, attract their customers to you, and boost your own revenue at little or no extra cost.

16

Final Thoughts

Making a million dollars was one of the easiest things I've ever done. Believing it could happen to me was one of the hardest.

—Matt Morris

When you don't know how to ride a bicycle, learning to steer and pedal without losing your balance can seem like the hardest thing in the world. After you learn, you may wonder how you ever thought it was difficult in the first place.

Believe it or not, that's the same feeling you'll get after you become a millionaire. Until you've gotten there, you may think it's nearly impossible. After you become a millionaire, you'll start asking, "Why did it take me so long?"

Without the right mind-set, practical techniques, and strategies, becoming a millionaire is, in fact, extremely difficult. But once you've uncovered these factors, I also know how easy it can really be. I know because I've been on both sides. I still remember all those sleepless nights in the backseat of my car, huddled under a dirty blanket because I couldn't afford to sleep in a cheap motel that night, and looking out the window, wondering, "How can someone like me, who can't even afford to take a shower every day, ever possibly become a millionaire?"

From where I sit today, I just have to smile at how far I've come and how far I still have to go. You see, we may be earning different amounts of money, but we're really on the same path, striving to achieve an even greater life for ourselves and our families. In this book, I've shared the most important strategies and foundational principles on becoming a millionaire. Now it's up to you to decide what to do with this information.

Because the tactical strategies can take some time to master, I've been asked over and over to provide business coaching to help entrepreneurs speed up their learning curve and to help walk them step-by-step through the process of getting a business off the ground. I've resisted this for years, but because I'm looking for a small number of success stories for my next book, I've decided to open up a coaching program to a limited number of entrepreneurs.

Those who create success stories of going from startup to millionaire will be those selected to be in my upcoming book and possibly an infomercial we're planning. If you're interested in being part of this private group, you can apply at www.MattMorris.com/coaching.

I know you want a better life for yourself. I know you want more choices. I can tell you right now that money isn't everything; it won't buy happiness and it won't buy peace or self-esteem. The real riches in life don't come in the form of dollar bills or gold bullion. Instead, the real riches in life come from taking that first leap of faith and believing in yourself. When you can honestly believe that you have what it takes to be more than you are right now, you'll already be halfway toward achieving your dreams, whatever they might be.

I'm here to tell you that you can do anything you want, but you must first make the commitment to do it and then decide that nothing will get in your way. The biggest obstacles blocking our path don't come from other people, the economy, or the environment, but from our own thoughts right between our ears. The moment you realize that the only one holding you back from your dreams is you, you'll be free to release yourself from your limiting self-image and truly grow into the man or woman you were meant to be.

The best and most exciting part of your life doesn't lie in your past or some distant future, but in the present. What you decide to do in every moment determines what will happen the rest of your life. You have the power to change your life in a split second. I know it won't seem easy at the time and you may get discouraged and lose faith along the way, but the next time you get depressed or feel like you just can't get back up on your feet again, think of me standing under the downpour in a church parking lot, trying to take a shower in a rainstorm. Think of me bathing in gas station bathrooms and say to yourself, "If *THAT* guy can do it, I **KNOW** I can!"

In Summary

Let's review the main points of this book. In the first part, I laid down the mental foundation you need before you can achieve anything. I explained the right way to set goals and gave you the exact steps that I use to keep myself organized and on track.

I didn't climb out of homelessness by myself. I surrounded myself with positive, affirmative people. If I couldn't find those types of people in my life, I listened to audio courses and read motivational books so even if I couldn't physically be with positive people, I could fill my thoughts and my life with their words and voices.

There's no way I could have succeeded without the help of so many other people, both friends and family members. I also couldn't have succeeded without the voices of so many speakers and trainers who showed me the way out of my despair in those days when I could barely scrape up enough money to buy myself something to eat.

You don't have to strive to become a millionaire all by yourself. There are literally millions of millionaires. Most of them are more than willing to share with you their tips and advice for how they succeeded and how you can, too. Success is only a secret to those who don't seek out the strategies to get there.

In the second part of the book, I gave you specific strategies for how to take yourself from trading hours for dollars to finding a business model that you can use as your vehicle for taking you from where you are right now and pulling you up to where you really want to be.

Each business model I covered has turned countless people into millionaires. Some took longer than others to get there, but none of them were required to have any special training or education to achieve it. All you need is a burning desire to succeed and an optimistic outlook that keeps you moving forward even when everything around you seems to be falling apart.

No matter who you are, where you live, or what your current situation might be, you can apply any of these strategies to get yourself out of debt and into building true wealth for yourself and your family.

If you're stuck in a job you don't like because it's not what you really want to do or because it takes away all your time, you don't have to stay there. I'm not telling you to quit your job just yet, but I am telling you to spend some time rearranging the priorities in your life so you can free yourself from the confines of a job as quickly as possible. Use your job to fund your success education and to teach you the skills you'll need to run your own business.

Although I've made millions through my own businesses, I don't want to give you the false illusion that it's going to be easy. You will certainly face challenges in running your own business. Expect these challenges and embrace them for the lessons they'll teach you. Each lesson pushes you closer to your goal. Sometimes the best lessons are disguised as failures. Always keep in mind that the reward for success is always worth the challenges you have to overcome.

Read this book as often as necessary. Mark it up with a pencil. Highlight certain paragraphs with a yellow marker. Do whatever it takes to get you on a path that will lead you to your dreams. Don't worry about the fear. Everyone is afraid, but it all boils down to one question, "How badly do you want it?" When you want it badly enough, as Susan Jeffers says in the title of her famous book, you'll *"Feel the fear and do it anyway."*

Each time you break through your fears, you'll start to realize something amazing. Obstacles keep popping up and fears keep frightening you, but each time you face them, they hold less and less control over your life. One day, you'll realize that they are no longer the ten foot boogeyman you thought they were, but just simple problems that only need an answer that you are perfectly capable of finding by yourself.

The more you step out of your comfort zone, the larger your comfort zone becomes. I think of comfort zones like a rubber band that won't pop. Maybe you've done this . . .when you stretch out a rubber band, it contracts back to its original size; or at least that's the way it appears. But the rubber band is actually a tiny bit larger because you stretched it. You might not notice it at first, but as you continue stretching the rubber band more and more, you see that it's actually expanded to the point that it will not contract back to its original shape. It's the same with your comfort zone. If you simply keep stretching it, what once frightened you will become an insignificant factor.

The mind, once expanded to the dimensions of larger ideas, never returns to its original size.

—Oliver Wendell Holmes

A Tale of Two Frogs

A group of frogs were traveling through the woods and two of them fell into a deep pit. All the other frogs gathered around the pit. When they saw how deep the pit was, they told the unfortunate frogs they would never get out. The two frogs ignored the comments and tried to jump up and out of the pit.

The other frogs kept telling them to stop, that they were as good as dead. Finally, one of the frogs took heed to what the other frogs were saying and simply gave up. He fell down and died. The other frog continued to jump as hard as he could. Once again, the crowd of frogs yelled at him to stop the pain and suffering and just die. He jumped even harder and finally made it out.

When he got out, the other frogs asked him, "Why did you continue jumping? Didn't you hear us?" The frog explained to them that he was hard of hearing, almost deaf. He thought they were encouraging him the entire time.

This story teaches two lessons:

1. There is power of life and death in the tongue. An encouraging word to someone who is down can lift that person up and help him or her make it through the day.
2. A destructive word to someone who is down can be what it takes to kill him or her. Be careful of what you say. Speak life to those who cross your path.

It is sometimes hard to understand that an encouraging word can go such a long way. Anyone can speak words that tend to rob another of the spirit to continue in difficult times. Special is the individual who will take the time to encourage another. Be special to others.

You have more power than you realize. Through this book, I hope to awaken you so you'll know how much power you really do have. My biggest wish for you is that you'll go on to achieve enormous success so that I can one day learn from you. The biggest reward for a mentor is when his or her students become the teacher.

I know that that these principles and strategies, along with your persistence and determination, will allow you to create a life of total abundance, a life of total wealth and a life of everything you've dreamed about.

Getting Started as an Unemployed Millionaire

If you want to become an Unemployed Millionaire, first accept the fact that you will have to change part of your life, whether it means taking less time to socialize at night or staying up one or more hours at night. The key to any business model you choose is to treat it like a business.

Put in consistent effort, however much time you can spare. When I started out, I put in time almost every night and over the weekends while I was working full-time. It wasn't necessarily easy, but because I was passionate about achieving my dreams, it never seemed like hard work. To me, hard work was staying stuck in a job that I knew would never allow me to achieve my dreams.

Accept the fact that you will have to change to become an Unemployed Millionaire. Carve out a schedule to get started on your business. It doesn't matter if you can only put in 10 hours a week. Putting in 10 hours of consistent effort every week is far better than putting in spurts of activity and then stopping for a period of time. You must develop the habit of consistent action toward achieving your goals.

Second, make sure you are passionate about what you're doing. The rewards go to people who enjoy themselves in the present while working toward a better future at the same time. As long as you're following your passion, no obstacle will ever be insurmountable.

Third, remain committed to your dreams. The more you keep your eye on your goals and your purpose for achieving them, the more you'll persist in making them a reality. Remember, you can't win if you ever quit. As long as you keep working toward your goal, you'll always be a winner in your own eyes.

What Is Your Calling?

I want you to think about something that I believe is deep within you. I believe everyone, including you, has a calling in life. Somewhere inside of you is a calling to do something great with your life. You may have been ignoring it for years. You may have spent the last few years caught in your normal routine of just getting by; nonetheless, your calling is there.

That calling is begging you to break free from your routine. To get out of your rut. To get out of mediocrity. The calling eats at you. It's the voice deep down in your gut that wants more. It's that voice you hear when you want to take your family on an exotic vacation, but you can't afford it. It's that voice you hear when you're at a restaurant and you have to look at the price before you look at the item to see if you can afford it. It's the voice you hear when you see someone *else* who is admired for doing great things in the world, and you realize you could do more.

You were not put on this earth for mediocrity. You were put on this earth to achieve your destiny. God has given you the power to achieve great heights, the power to make a difference in the world, and the power to realize your dreams. My core belief in life is that we were all given the exact same God-given ability on Earth. How we manifest those abilities, however, is up to us.

Unfortunately, too many people live their lives filled with excuses like, "I'm not smart enough, I don't have enough education, I'm too poor, I'm too old," or even the one I used for years, "I'm too young"—all lies we use as excuses to live small. Whether you want to admit this about yourself or not, you were created with all the creativity, all the genius, all the determination, and all the strength that you need to create a truly remarkable life.

I'm expecting big things from you and I hope so much that we have the chance to meet in person one day soon when you can tell me about the amazing life you created for yourself. Take that first step now. The rest of your life is waiting to see what you're going to do.

Far better is to dare mighty things, to win glorious triumphs, even though checkered by failure, than to take ranks with those poor spirits who neither enjoy much nor suffer much, because they live in the gray twilight of mediocrity that knows neither victory nor defeat.

—Theodore Roosevelt

Acknowledgments

The writing of this book would never have been possible if not for the support of a large group of understanding and supportive people. There are those I'm sure I'll miss. Please know it wasn't intentional and I do thank you.

First and foremost, thank you to my beautiful wife Rhonda, who put up with countless nights of me holed up in my office writing until the early hours of the morning and through the weekends all while she kept our family and household running smoothly. You are truly an amazing woman. A big thank you also goes to your wonderful parents, Roger and Nadia Salah, who helped out so much while I was busy writing and during my travels.

This book would not have been possible without the assistance of Wallace Wang. Your creativity, research, editing, and endless hours on the phone with me made this book a reality. You are an absolute pleasure and joy to work with. Thanks to my agent, Bill Gladstone, who is the best in the business. Thank you for your faith in me from the moment we first met.

A huge thank you goes to Jimmy Bellew, to whom I owe much of my success. Jimmy has been my right-hand man and incredible friend for nearly a decade. Over the years he's put up with all my crazy ideas and found ways to make them work. He's been the rock behind our companies. Jimmy, I never could have done it without you. A special thanks to Kent Huie, who has always gone above and beyond to manage our customer support, operations, and many other parts of the business. Thank you to my wonderful assistant, Amy Garrett, without whom I would be completely lost. I owe the entire corporate team much more thanks than I have space to give here so please know I thank you all tremendously.

Thank you to Johnny Wimbrey, Kalpesh Patel, Ned and Cheryl Rae, Soojay and Casandra Devraj, Trisha Smith, and Nik Halik. Your leadership in building our business around the world has been amazing and your friendship is cherished. You are all amazing leaders and I'm so blessed to have you in my life.

Thank you to Mary Beth Harris for stepping out of your comfort zone to introduce me to the world of free enterprise. I hope our paths cross again one day. Thank you to Wayne Nugent, who became my mentor the day I met him. Wayne's mentorship and influence have given me an amazing life. Thank you to the countless speakers and trainers who have been instrumental in my development. There are too many to mention all of them but a special thank you goes to Les Brown and Tony Robbins for the amazing difference you have made in my life.

Thank you to my mother, who taught me that to get what you want in life you have to be aggressive. The assertiveness lesson you taught me when I was about 10 years old was one of the greatest lessons of my life. Watching you go after your dreams, despite the struggles and hardships, gave me the inspiration to go after mine. To my 19-year-old brother Shawn, I'm so proud of you and can't wait to see the huge success that you'll become. Go after your dreams with everything you have! To my grandmothers and the rest of my family, thank you for your endless love.

Finally, thank you to my daughter, Zara, whose birth coincided with the completion of this book. You have given me fulfillment beyond what I ever dreamed was possible. I've never seen anything as perfect as your smiling face. I promise to always support you in your dreams and goals and to be the best Daddy I can be.

Index

Acquire This Name, 143, 144
Action management, 63–75
  creating wants list with, 68–69
  and ego management, 65–66
  and e-mail addiction, 73–74
  prioritizing with, 69–71
  and scheduling, 72–73
  setting time limits with, 71–72
  and time management, 64
  and your values, 66–68
Action plans, 58–62
Adams, John Quincy, 76
Advertising:
  banner, 204–205
  Ezine, 164–165
  of other people's products, 151–153
Affiliate marketing, 153–154, 201–203.
    See also Pay-per-performance (PPP)
    advertising
Affiliate Tips, 154
Affordable Programmers, 149
Afternic, 143
Agents of Value, 161, 194
Alexa toolbar, 208–209
All You Can Do Is All You Can Do
  (Art Williams), 44
Amazon.com, 145, 155, 167, 220
Amway, 123
Antin, Brad, 226
AOL Video, 114
Apple Inc., 219, 225
Ariely, Dan, 222
Article City, 160
Article Directory, 160
Article marketing, 160–161
Articles, 234

The Art of War (Sun Tzu), 112–113
AssistU, 197
AT&T, 219
Attitude control, 87–88
Auctions, online, see Online auctions
Avon, 123
Aweber, 171
Azoogle, 154

Bandwagon effect, 232–233
Bank of America, 178
Banner advertising, 204–205
Banners Mall, 205
Bannister, Roger, 89–90
Base Camp, 192
Belief(s), 28–42
  and controlling your mind, 30–33
  experiences shaping our, 33–36
  and faith, 29–30
  and law of consistency, 39–42
  of other people, 36–38
  and power of lies, 38
  and subconscious thought, 38
  and success, 97
Best Jobs Philippines, 197
Better Business Bureau, 232
Bid 4 Assets, 179
Bidz, 137
Bill and Melinda Gates Foundation, 46
Bismarck, Otto von, 108
BloggingStocks, 155
Blogs, 155
Body language, 79
Boing Boing, 155
Bonnano, Margaret, 63
Box Shot 3D, 168

Branding, 115
Break.com, 154
Bribery, ethical, 220–224
Brick and mortar businesses, 22–23, 112, 134, 193
Brickwork India, 194
Brown, Les, xi–xiii, 17
Buffet, Warren, 46
Business, starting a, *see* Starting a business
Business cards, 165
Business strategies for unemployed millionaires, 17–27
  businesses benefiting from, 24–25
  philosophy of, 18
  and time vs. money, 19–23
  and wealth foundation, 26–27
Butler, Nicolas M., 50
Buy Domains, 143, 144
Buying decisions, 225–229

Caples, John, 205
Carroll, Lewis, 54
CastingWords, 167
Centerpointe Research Institute, 226
Certified Financial Planner Board of Standards, 26
Challenges, 98–100
Change, 105–106
Chase Mortgage, 178
Children, 49
Chitika, 153
Churchill, Winston, 87
CitiGroup, 106
ClickBank, 154
Click-through rate (CTR), 164
Click tracking, 202
Commission Junction, 154
Commissions, referral, 120
Competition, 108–118, 218–235
  and buying decisions, 225–229
  and establishing trust, 229–233
  and ethical bribery, 220–224
  and expertise, 234–235
  Bill Gates and, 109
  learning from, 112
  and lower prices, 218–220
  and modeling, 110–111

and personalized service, 224–225
unique selling propositions for, 115–118
Competitive intelligence, 112–115
Computers, 68, 86, 225
Confidence:
  consumer, 122
  and leadership, 78–81
  and success, 41
Consistency, law of, 39–42
Consumer confidence, 122
Contact information, 233
Content-oriented Web sites, 155
Contribute, 149
Controlling your mind, 30–33
Coolidge, Calvin, 92
Cost per acquisition (CPA) network, 153–154
Countrywide, 178
CPA network, *see* Cost per acquisition network
Craftsman, 118
Credibility seals, 232–233
Crime statistics, 183
CTR (click-through rate), 164
Current events, 162
CurrentForeclosures.com, 178

"Daily four," 190–191
Decision making, 90–91
Designers, web page, 148–149
Desire:
  and dreams, 44–46
  and false illusions, 44–46
Dieting, 39
Digital products:
  selling of, 166–168
  shipping of, 135
Directory of Ezines, 165
Doing, trying vs., 49–50
Domain names, 142–145
Domino's Pizza, 116–117
DoubleYourDating.com, 170
Dreams, 42–53
  and desire, 44–46
  of leaders, 82–84
  lifetime dream list, 51–53
  of Alfred Nobel, 46–48

and success, 48–49
and trying vs. doing, 49–50
Dreamweaver, 148–149
Drop-shippers, 139–140
Drucker, Peter F., 187

eBay, 135, 137–139, 145
e-books, 166–167, 221
E-Commerce stores, 145–147
Economic crisis:
   and network marketing, 122–123
   and real estate investing, 178–179
   and risk, 106
Edison, Thomas, 90–91
Edison Universal Stock Printer, 91
Education, 4, 106–107
Ego management, 65–66
Einstein, Albert, 133
Elance, 149, 161, 194
E-mail:
   addiction to, 73–74
   signature files embedded in, 159–160
E-mail copy, 205
E-mail lists, 168–172
E-mail newsletters, 161–162
Emotions, 87
Ethical bribery, 220–224
Exact Target, 172
Experiences, 33–36
Expertise, 234–235
Eye contact, 79–80
Ezinead.net, 165
Ezine advertising, 164–165
EzineAdvertising.com, 165
Ezine Articles, 160, 234

Failure, 90–91, 128
Faith, 29–30
False illusions, 98–100
Families, 85
Fark.com, 154
Fat Cow, 147
Federal Express (FedEx), 116, 118
Feed the Children, 104
Finder's fees, 182
Firefox, 208
Flipping (real estate), 179–180
Ford, Henry, 119

Foreclosure, 178–179
Foreclosures.com, 179
Franklin, Ben, 9
Fuller Brush, 123

Gates, Bill, 86, 109
General Motors, 106
Get Friday, 197
Get Response, 171
Gifts, 216–217
Gizmodo, 155
Glickman, Louis, 173
Global Sky, 197
Goal setting, 54–62
   and action plans, 58–62
   and motivation behind goals, 58
   and specific goals, 56–57
   and subconscious thought, 55, 57
GoArticles, 160
GoDaddy, 144
Google, 156–159, 162–164, 208–209
Google AdSense, 152–153
Google Adwords, 205
Google Docs, 191–192
Google Video, 114
GoToMeeting, 197
Gratitude, 99
Great Domains, 143, 144
Greetings, 79
Guarantees, 225–228
Guru.com, 161

Hahn, Fred E., 205
Handshakes, 79
Handwritten notes, 217
Hare Krishnas, 223–224
Harris, Bill, 226
Hershey's Kisses, 222
Hoffman, Dustin, 30
Holmes, Oliver Wendell, 240
Host Gator, 147
Hosting (Web site), 147–151
Host Monster, 147
Host Upon, 147
Hotel suites, 177
How to Write a Good Advertisement
   (Victor O. Schwab), 205

HTML Source Code, 158
Hunger crisis, 103–104

IBM, 34, 90, 109
iContact, 171
Identity, 32
Indirect competitors, 113
InfusionSoft, 203
Ingram Micro, 140
Integrity:
    and leadership, 91–92
    of networking marketing companies,
        130–131
Intelligence, competitive, *see* Competitive
    intelligence
International Association of Virtual
    Assistants, 197
Internet Explorer, 208
Internet Girl Friday, 197
Internet marketing, 133–172
    ads on web sites for, 154–159
    and advertising other people's
        products, 151–153
    and affiliate marketing, 153–154
    and article marketing, 160–161
    creating a web site for, 141–145
    creating e-Commerce stores through
        third parties for, 145–147
    e-mail lists for, 168–172
    e-mail newsletters for, 161–162
    and Ezine advertising, 164–165
    getting started in, 105
    hosting and building a web site for,
        147–151
    mail-order marketing vs., 133–134
    and online auctions, 136–141
    and recruiting affiliates, 165–166
    and search engine optimization,
        156–159
    and search engine pay-pay-click
        advertising, 162–164
    selling digital products with, 166–168
    and shipping digital products, 135
    and signature files, 159–160
    success of, 34–35
Internet Movie Database, 151
Inventory, 134
iPhoto, 219
iWeb, 149

Jeffers, Susan, 239
Joint venturing, 200–217
    and banner advertising, 204–205
    and e-mail copy, 205
    and formula for recruiting partners,
        207–215
    and maintaining relationships, 215–217
    mistakes made in, 203–204
    and search engine pay-pay-click
        advertising, 205–207
    and starting affiliate programs,
        201–203
Jones, Frances, 104
Jones, Larry, 104

Keller, Helen, 84
Kennedy, Dan, 205
Keywords, 162–164
Kiyosaki, Robert, 121
Kroc, Ray, 218

Law of consistency, 39–42
Law of reciprocity, 223–224
Leadership, 76–94
    and confidence, 78–81
    and decision making, 90–91
    and dreams of leaders, 82–84
    inspiring vision through, 84–86
    and integrity, 91–92
    and network marketing, 129
    of Wayne Nugent, 77–78
    and persistence, 92–93
    setting examples with, 88–90
    and superior attitudes, 87–88
    and taking responsibility, 94
Leasing options, 180–181
LibriVox, 166
Lies:
    power of, 38
    and subconscious, 57
Lifehacker.com, 155
Lifetime dream list, 51–53, 74
Lindt, 222
LinkShare, 154
Local businesses, 112
Logic, 83
Lombardi, Vince, 44, 88
LookSmart, 153
Lower prices, 218–220

Lucas, George, 25
Lyris, 172

McAfee Secure, 232
McDonald's, 126–127
Mail-order marketing, 133–134
Mal's e-Commerce, 151
Management, 187–199. *See also* Action
    management
    "daily four" for, 190–191
    master project list for, 191–192
    and outsourcing, 193–196
    of staff, 188–189
    with virtual assistants, 196–199
    weekly accountability meetings for,
    193
Mandela, Nelson, 82
Marine Corps, 99
Marketing. *See also* Internet marketing;
    Network marketing
    article, 160–161
    mail-order, 133–134
    traditional, 120
MarketingGenerator.net, 170
Market Leverage, 154
Mary Kay, 123
Master project lists, 191–192
Master reseller rights, 166–167
Material possessions, 46
Max Covers, 168
MCI, 219
Meetings, weekly accountability,
    193
Mentors, 131–132
Meta tags, 157–158
Microsoft, 86, 109, 219
Microsoft adCenter, 153
Microsoft Disk Operation System
    (MS-DOS), 109
Microsoft Expression Web, 149
MLS, *see* Multiple Listing Service
Modeling:
    and competition, 110–111
    concept of, 12
Money, 19–23
Morris, Matt, 28, 200, 236
Motivation:
    behind goals, 58
    with leadership, 85–86

MS-DOS (Microsoft Disk Operation
    System), 109
MSN Live Search, 156
Multiple Listing Service (MLS), 178, 182

Name Boy, 143
Netflix, 113
Network marketing, 119–132
    basics of, 124–125
    and economic crisis, 122–123
    finding a mentor for, 131–132
    finding companies that specialize in,
    127–129
    getting started with, 105
    mistakes made in, 130
    opinions on, 121
    planting season of, 125–126
    traditional vs., 120
Network Solutions, 143
Never Blue, 154
New Year's resolutions, 106
Nightingale, Earl, xvii
Nitroglycerine, 47
Nitro-Traffic.com, 170
Nobel, Alfred, 46–48
No money down techniques, 181–182
Nordstrom, 224–225
North American Wholesale Co-Op
    Association, 141
Nugent, Wayne, 77–78
Nvu, 148–149

Odesk, 194, 197
1 and 1 Internet, 143, 144, 147
1 Shopping Cart, 151, 202
Onion.com, 151
Online auctions, 136–141
Open Directory Project, 156
Outlaw, Frank, 42
Outsourcing, 193–196
Overstock, 137

Passion:
    as basis for starting a business, 100–104
    starting a business based on your, 242
PayPal, 141
Pay-per-click (PPC) advertising, 151–152
Pay-per-performance (PPP) advertising,
    151–153

PDAs (Personal Digital Assistants), 68
PDF (Portable Document Format), 167
Persistence:
  and leadership, 92–93
  and network marketing, 130
Personal development industry, 48–49, 54, 103
Personal Digital Assistants (PDAs), 68
Personalized service, 224–225
PHPCareer.com, 194
Physiology, 80
Planting season, of network marketing, 125–126
Plimu, 154
Portable Document Format (PDF), 167
Posture, 80
Power of asking, 176–177
PPC advertising, *see* Pay-per-click advertising
PPP advertising, *see* Pay-per-performance advertising
Predictably Irrational (Dan Ariely), 222
Prices, 218–220
Prioritized Daily Task List (PDTL), 68
Prioritizing:
  with action management, 69–71
  for management, 190–191
Privacy policies, 233
Profit, 175
Project Gutenburg, 166
ProStores, 145
Public domain, 166
PutFile, 114

Quick Base, 192

Radio, 235
RapidWeaver, 149
Rare items, 139
Real Estate Disposition Corporation, 179
Real estate investing, 173–184
  benefits of, 173–174
  and economic crisis, 178–179
  flipping and renting with, 179–180
  getting started in, 105, 182–184
  leasing options with, 180–181
  making an immediate profit with, 175

  no money down techniques for, 181–182
  and power of asking, 176–177
Realty Trac, 179
Reciprocity, law of, 223–224
Recruiting affiliates, 165–166, 207–215
Redbox, 113
Referral commissions, 120
Religious beliefs, 32
Rent a Coder, 149, 194
Renting, 179–180
Responsibility, 94
Rich Dad, Poor Dad (Robert Kiyosaki), 121
Risks, 106–107
Robbins, Tony, 11–12
Rockefeller, John D., 86
ROI Rocket, 154
Roosevelt, Eleanor, 91
Roosevelt, Theodore, 90, 243
Ruskin, John, 3

Scheduling, 72–73
Schwab, Victor O., 205
Schweitzer, Albert, 97
ScriptLance, 149
Search engine optimization (SEO), 156–159
Search engine pay-pay-click advertising:
  and Internet marketing, 162–164
  and joint venturing, 205–207
Sedo, 143
Selective price cutting, 220
SEO, *see* Search engine optimization
Shaklee, 123
ShareASale, 154
Shaw, George Bernard, 93
Sheep mentality, 77
Shopping cart software, 150–151
Signature files, 159–160
Signatures, 233
Significance, of work, 65–66
Silverpop, 172
Social proof, 230
Spielberg, Steven, 25
Sprint, 219
Squeeze pages, 170
Staff, 188–189

Starting a business, 97–107
  and committing to change, 105–106
  and false illusions, 98–100
  passion as basis for, 100–104
  and risks, 106–107
Stress, 65
Subconscious thought:
  and beliefs, 38
  and goal setting, 55, 57
Success:
  and dreams, 48–49
  formula for, 31
  in network marketing, 130
Success University, 103, 232
Sugarman, Joe, 205
Sun Tzu, 112–113

Television, 235
Template Monster, 148
Templates Box, 148
Template World, 148
Tested Advertising Methods (John Caples
  and Fred E. Hahn), 205
Testimonials, 230–231
3d Cart, 151
Time, 19–23
  limits on, 71–72
  management of, 64
Traditional marketing, 120
Transcriptions Service, 167
Triggers (Joe Sugarman), 205
Trump, Donald, 121
Trust, 229–233
Truste, 232
Trying, doing vs., 49–50
Tupperware, 123
The Twilight Zone, 43

UBid, 137
The Ultimate Sales Letter (Dan Kennedy),
  205
Unique selling propositions (USPs),
  115–118
United Country Auction Services, 179
United Parcel Service (UPS), 116
U.S. Department of Labor, 106–107
USPs, *see* Unique selling propositions

Vacations, 19
Value, 162
Values, 66–68
Verisign, 232
Viddler, 114
VideoGeneratorSoftware.com, 170
Video hosting sites, 114
VidiLife, 114
Virtual assistants, 196–199
Virtual Assistants, Inc., 197
Virtual Assistants for You, 197
Virtual Cover Creator, 168
Vision, 84–86
Voice, 80
Volusion, 151

Wag the Dog, 30
Wal-Mart, 112, 117–118, 219, 224
Wants list, 68–69
Warning ads, 163
Watson, Thomas, 34, 90
Wealth foundation, 26–27
Web Design Solutions, 149
Web page designers, 148–149
Web sites:
  ads on, 154–159
  creating, 141–145
  hosting and building, 147–151
  sales through, 110–111
Website Templates, 148
Weekly accountability meetings, 193
Western Union, 91
WhoIs.net, 210–211
Wholesale Central, 141
Williams, Art, 44
Williams & Williams, 179
Wimbrey, Johnny, 125
Windows Photo Gallery, 219
Word of mouth advertising, 165
Workaholics4Hire, 194
Work culture, 189
Work Zone, 192
Worldwide Brands, 140

Yahoo!, 114, 145, 156, 163
Yew, Lee Kuan, 193
YouTube, 114

How to Claim Your FREE Downloadable CD Package With Other Unemployed Millionaires – $97 Value!

As a special bonus with the purchase of this book, I've assembled a collection of private interviews with other Unemployed Multi-Millionaires. You'll receive over six hours of no-holds-barred, down and dirty strategies that these entrepreneurs have used to create fortunes.

Here is just a small sampling of what you'll learn:

- **How a 17-year old kid started earning $15,000 per day online**
- How someone on welfare became the 25th wealthiest person in America amassing a billion dollar net worth
- **How a former drug dealer earned over $100,000 in only four months – legally!**
- The strategies a coal-mine worker used to generate a six-figure passive residual income
- **How a struggling salesman earned his first million dollars online**
- Much More!

You'll learn all that and more when you follow the steps to claim your $97 gift:

Step 1 – Go to this URL:
www.MattMorris.com/freegift

Step 2 – Authenticate
You will be prompted to open the book to a certain page and then find a particular word. This is our way of verifying that you purchased the book.

Step 3 – Enjoy!
You'll be emailed the downloadable CDs and will also receive my personal contact information should you have any questions for me or my team.

I look forward to hearing your success story!

Matt Morris
Author, *The Unemployed Millionaire*

P.S. – As a special added bonus, while space is still available, you'll receive a free 30-minute private coaching session with one of our certified business experts. Whether you're looking to start a new business or looking to take your business to the next level, my team has helped hundreds of entrepreneurs create wildly successful businesses.